AF322656

GYPSIES

OF THE UNATTAINABLE

C.P. BYRON

Published by Rock Drill Press

Jacket Art: Hieronymus Bosch *Garden of Earthly Delights* (detail) 1490-1510
Rock Drill logo: Line art of Jacob Epstein's *Torso in Metal from Rock Drill.* 1916

Interior art: Cleo Damianakes. *Allegretto.* Etching on woven paper, (1922)
Photo of C.P. Byron: Gabriel Paris River. Paris December, (2015)
Back cover photo: Bea Beckhon-Dhense. Ocracoke Island, (2020)

Pre-press production by Holbrook Author Services. Portsmouth, NH.
Text Layout in Michelangelo BQ and Aldus LT Std.

First Edition

ISBN: 9798330272891

for

H

« Mes amis, je veux qu'elle soit reine! » « Je veux être reine! »
Elle riait et tremblait.

— Arthur Rimbaud

I sense the echo of a voice
I do not hear,
I am not sure the breath I hold
Is mine.

— Marion Strobel

I felt that I was leaving part of myself behind, and that
wherever I went afterwards I should feel the lack of it,
and search for it hopelessly…

— Evelyn Waugh

GYPSIES

OF THE UNATTAINABLE

PARIS POEMS

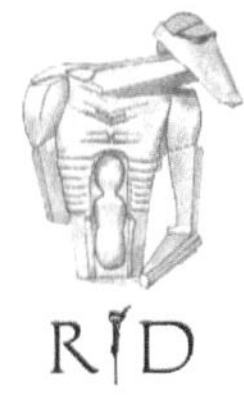

PARIS   BOSTON

Poems

Section 1 : La Bonaparte

Section 2 : La Palette

Section 3 : La Contrescarpe

Section 5 : Le Champs de Mars

Coda : The Worm's Art

C.P. Byron Biography

Preface

Gypsies of the Unattainable is a selection Rolleiflex prints, wrote C.P. Byron of his labyrinthine epic. Noting Ezra Pound's remark that "All ages are contemporaneous..." Byron sought to present Purgatory not as myth, but as the streets we walk each day of our lives. These poems portray irrevocable decisions made flesh, the irreducible sum of all our choices, Byron concluded. The wandering poet's records reveal themselves throughout his long Paris cycle.

With Homeric and Dantean references in structure and in progression, the cycle's prime influence, however, must be attributed to Ovid's ethopoeia, rendered by Byron as personal and intimate character sketches. It is this use of character portraiture that carries weight and conveys meaning in each of the poems. Even the most prominent missing character, the artist, appears as in Vermeer's masterpieces of camera obscura. In *Gypsies*, the poet presents and explores his vast and varied cast by allowing us to see them in their most profound intimacies — sometimes shocking, occasionally banal — until we all but inhabit their circles of acquaintances. We are sometimes embarrassed for them until our embarrassment dissipates unawares into the heady air of the human, the humane, and the often inhumane, Byron ushers us into the Purgatory of modern European life as seen through the eyes and heard in the voices of expatriates past and present a full century after Gertrude Stein's infamous Lost Generation.

What are we to make of today's sojourning, go-go breed Anthony Burgess described as Infernal Man, Purgatorial Man, Paradisal Man? Through its nine sections and posthumous poems spanning Europe, America, South America, and Asia, *Gypsies* ferries travelers on a time-unbound odyssey in search of emotional richness, intellectual precision, and spiritual meaning — descent, transcendence, and transfiguration.

Are the voices echoing upward through the labyrinth mine? players ask between lines. Is Paradise possible in the Quantum Age of the Anthropocene? Is grace yet attainable? These and other questions await us, but as a certain Mr. Barnes replied, brooding over his eviscerated soul in the back of his own fictional Parisian taxi, "Isn't it pretty to think so?"

Discursive, spiraling, yet strangely linear to the end, with so many introductions made both in Byron's perpetual now, *Gypsies of the Unattainable* is fiction truer than true life, as is every human life, including one's own.

Tu lascerai ogne cosa diletta più caramente;
e questo è quello strale che l'arco de lo
essilio pria saetta.
　　　　　— Dante (*Cacciaguida, Paradiso 17)*

I shall know you, secrets
by the litter you have left
and by your bloody foot-prints.
　　　　　— Lola Ridge

He cannot tell the rate at which he travels backwards.
　　　　　— Elizabeth Bishop

They were never there. You and I, we were there. Just over there.

Here.

Gypsies of the Unattainable

Σα βγεις στον πηγαιμό για την Ιθάκη,
να εύχεσαι νάναι μακρύς ο δρόμος,
γεμάτος περιπέτειες, γεμάτος γνώσεις.

—Konstantínos Pétrou Kaváfis

ONE

AN INCONVENIENT WOMAN

Once my love had the lion's mouth,
My breasts were the pillars of the south.
                    — *Edith Sitwell*

I *have lost the feeling of my pleasure,* she grieves each breath
from her plush seat by the Crillon's crazed bar.
Mislaid names of colours, their splendid otherness; no longer believe
mere hope shall do to cull vain fictions from a scurrilous death.

You were heroic to cope, to hold, *the man pales*
una gran donna, no raving girl, nor feral cat, *his cautious coax.*
She pauses, draws a second unfiltered cigarette, tapping
her Gauloises against the helmeted wings of its blue box.

Scowling, she holds it in her stale and overstated mouth
fills the room with spiral vortices, feline eyes over-styled.
Bright Camparis flash, signal scattered refuse, ruined truths.
Thwarted, mes plaisirs sacrés, mon faux Graal...that futile guile.

Our luncheons were adorned with rarest treasure, *he mourns.*
I've lost the feeling of my pleasure, she shudders, sainted, then smiles.

Nude Descending A Stair

George V. Thick skulled, tongue-dull, an infidel
dodges deftly behind a woman's plodding trust.
Does a cuckquean taste no alien breath in barley lungs?

He sweats a girl from every pore. How many days
more does she imagine he can afford
this latest regret, unwary girl? *His new whore…*

Blonde, leggy, she reads de Beauvoir to pass
time, buys his Edradour, pours his glass;
at his club's bar, he describes the heart-shaped ass

recounting trysts at the top of umbrous stairs
after drinks at Intermezzo.
She knows, of course, but is raw, needy

supported by a nervous, Yellow Pages analyst
whose daughter sticks her unmade head in gas
when the lesbian despair will not stop

who drops her practice and flies to Chicago
saving the blue-faced child while clients split
apart, refracted Duchamp women descending

in contorted cubist portraits without accord.
Tiens… Between bed and phone, she thinks,
Regardes — my poor, puff-breasted boor.

This cock's proud cluck has not been said
which sounds the dread to come when I
pluck off its smug, red-tufted head.

METIS IN MALAKOFF DREAMS OF ATHENA

Woman is part less than human, part more
than human and part human.
— Susan Taubes

In a whelk-footed bath, shell-pink Metis brushes her skin gold
twists plastic strips about her Oceanid mouth; breathes, drowning
deeply until her warder-lover comes, clutching to retrieve her.

Carried to her memory bed, she makes blank love. She weeps
tints of sea-gold washing under Malakoff. On tile white as bleach
he reaches her. He pleases, reforms her, teaches her.

They sleep; she dreams in the breach. Greedily, she dreams.
Long women leave the beach, hammer golden breastplates polished
in his belly, fired with clatter and gossip, all sheathed in gold.

Morning. She wakes, devoured, returns to Port de Chatillon
buys paint, strapping tape, long leaves of assuasive plastic wrap.
She shall be golden, black eyes blazon, *a metal sun, radiant — golden.*

Muriel

Not even pain has that precision
With which it struck in youth-time.
　　　　　　　— Mina Loy

Hermès foulards, heavy skeins of Romeo y Julietas flee
les fenetres hautes, lazy M's mounting indolently like American debt
over fin du siecle cornices, ornate frames above filthy scree
of gulls feeding from scarred, wet stones mortared with regret.

Tourists meet in tweeds; German autocars embark pale Swedes
carrying Leicas and lenses following their shoot in la Huechette.
Cursive scripts of cigarettes pen indifferently, *With Deepest Regret* —
Defeated, Eliot Paul takes the blow of a guide's tedious screed.

Close, refracted in tall windows, stood among a small salon's musty set
a man tracks languid shadows across the ceramic face of a tower clock.
Between decorous bridges, worn barges peel, blue *Bateaux Mouches* dock.
Traffic in knots, he listens for iron shod hooves of Republican Guards.

Weeks on, burnt stubs of Romeo y Julietas drop to an ashen moquette.
Arrete! he shrieks. She turns from Grands Augustins below; turns hard.

GIRL IN HIGH WINDOW

No costume unconcealing, so *de trop*
trop peu as is her laugh while she dances
half bidden behind parted curtains
above the brown Thames, darting
silhouette in full unpetalling
flowers unfolded for florid tourists.

Light-bodied, unhidden
                          pear-shaped
on legs long in immaculate rise
the gauzy *culotte*, the pale, plump
saucy-shapely-shifting round bottom
which leaves gaping all who apprise.
                                   One thinks

Kew, Kensington, Killesberg Parken
Octobers in Stuttgart, smooth-skinned
chestnuts and brown acorns the colours
of flesh, of heartbreaking eyes…

                            London's dirty
river drifts voyeurs and spies
secret trysts imagining
who uncover no schism, stealing
scenes from fantastical, fleeting
hedonistic games, flirty cinematic
frames, frame by frame
spare and sheer as linen.
                            Unusually unhurried
creased men abiding worried lives ride
narrow glass boats, pretend still to be
fleece-clad Normand hunters stalking
approaching by drizzly Battersea's new
power station, tube station.

                            Westminster neglected
Big Ben's pealing, Tower's moat
the distantly removed traffic's tintinnabulation
forgotten, plying against the anfractuous shore

their long-unpracticed, unaccustomed
wielding of borrowed force.

                    None ignore
bare bounce of breast, of course
nor her feline striding in a nonchalance so
vaguely unaware across an impossibly high
far floor, high window to high window
                                    the thrilling
sight unbearable in its dare, her delighted
heedless killing
                    Inviolata unyielding.

Le Select

In Le Select, you decried Rodin as fraud, petty thief
stealing Camille's man-tainted soul until, mad to be adored
mad, perhaps, for relief from a formlessness long deplored
she sculpted not in bronze but in metaled grief.

Yet, you snatch things rarer than her laboured belief.
Near Montparnasse, June rains steaming on Rue de Rennes
Luxembourg's lilacs, candles in Saint-Germain when
none come to pray. Worse, your sins are not so brief

as Camille's sadness. Vile as coy August's ferocious lies
joyless larcenist, feign no artlessness in cuts you devise.

MAN WITH BITCH IN PÈRE LACHAISE

Attendre. I long suspected we would round to this.
Listen... There, the callow mawing underground —
bloody, whimpering subterranean hound
paws at the muck of that awful abyss.

It pleads its walk with a humid, unctuous kiss
entreating for the leash. C'est l'enfer, but we were bound
to go. I'd thought we'd lost its lead, then found
the ragged thing when least expecting it. We miss

our walks together, I suppose; now claggy earth
compels we tread whence other curs have fled
save this old bitch, all tooth and bone, its hearth
lacking light or warmth, tangled clots of yew its bed.

Regardes. Cocks its head, hunts her heart, newly flown
unmoved by moon-blue irises, static as Attic stone.

Daum Figurines

Behind in-thrown casements down Gît-le-Cœur
hesitant hands chase Schubert's sonata 19 in C.
A chic couple pauses below, cranes, attends. He slows
watches her remember when she plotted, too, plodding
same on her treasured Pleyel in the flat on Saint-Louis

where he strolled into life. Up Saint-André-des-Arts
towards Café de Flore she begins to think, turning
Every life becomes a lesson in loss, a yearning
to bear one's failings, when he stops with a start
offering, *I think I understand what you were saying*

this morning, your greed for veracity
metaled logic, the perfect performance
a proof of transcendent mind unlike mine.
As he knew, her clever pale eyes would ever see
what his may never. (She leaves nothing to chance.)

At dusk, they pass Cauris, where often she shops
en route to La Palette, seeking fixity in Daum figurines.
One she spies, head between knees; the next, tightly curled
veils herself from view. At a third glass girl, she blocks.
Days, hours he unplots, yet does not unknot her ad hoc world.

GRANDS AUGUSTINS

Arcing amber halogens cross faux baroque ceilings
smart flats against the Seine, bobbing bateaux mouches
bring violet spots, burn the blue edges of a small Matisse.
On Pont des Arts, Japanese shooters flash, stealing

frames of French light for apartments in Kyoto, Hong Kong
while always, ever, incessant in ringing, great bells gong
along washed-out, weary quais breaking down
each frieze until every angle is bludgeoned slightly wrong,

beyond recognition, nearly. *Soudainement,* she understood.
Raw February sleet wrung relentless and without pity
angular sheets strung across the dirty and the good, hang
along a turgid Seine unretreating.
                    Edge of night city, dour
pickpocket of hearts, trafficker in lovers' grief, how willfully we
plunge under winter floods in these haunted, Hadean streets.

Blonde at Zénith

Life changes in the instant. The ordinary instant.
— Joan Didion

Haste of urgent, whippet-lean years as if race hares pressed
relentlessly since last in elegant club level cuts he undressed
her from satin buttons, the white linen blouse, then under
Armani curves on Balenciaga heels and Coco Chanel wonders.

Years, she recalls, in halls of distressed emptiness lapsed
between this night and what passed. It was so common a life, traps
of offices, private schools, *les boucheries, les jardins*
a friends' new wedding. In time, however, peccadilloes pardoned

form fracking lines at cracked corners of hydraulic eyes
revelations of deeper unhardenings having learned less to despise
his moving faultlessly, covering her subterranean bets, refusing
nothing; yet, sounder grown, the more disingenuous her musings.

Sundry slighter seasons hence, Marsallis blows a sinuous *"Skylark"*.
Lower balcony, a man suffused with light, a blonde pales dark.

After the Rijks

After the Rijks, his wife spoke. *I suppose we've misunderstood
history's manifest futility.* Room following high-ceilinged room
past fruitful stills in cavernous halls, she recalls
wind-blown and dashed, tumbling across polished floors, out
spinning doors, English lions in repose, and museum urns.

Husband: *What next East India Company, what sponsoring
corporate board shall fill these rooms with willful larcenies, what factories
might fly vainglorious art here two centuries hence? To whose untaxed
good end beyond bottom lines plumped towards quarterly releases?*
Silence. At once she knew. No demographic curve appeases.

Vuillard in a Paris salon. *He gives me pleasure,* she voiced.
The world turns uniformly, invariably in an inverse course
increments of unhappiness infinitesimally small, light and heavy
beyond measure. Later, over cocktails, she restarted
puzzling what steeper duty their bartered coming days will levy.

Sunday Morning with Mondrian

One gets it, *n'est-ce pas?* tethered along. Apprehends theory, Piet
but grows unfit — *paresseux?* — on the tedious approach
to such short ends, angled measures of a minimalist's subset.
So rigid, so cold — so strict! — this aesthetic code you coach.

Who doesn't grow tired, bent down bearing Tiresias's coal eyes?
I spy vast, barren, architectural planes
and pine in blithe naïveté for all you cajole us to revise.
Pretty Fragonard, say, not requiring introspective strain.

What you deny, all you shout out, the new you'd have us pounce
you got it just so — *nearly* so — but flat truths lack conviction.
O, who knows? A Turner. *Madame X.* That Constable you trounce
with your deadpan ripostes deploying such dry, geometric diction.

Verily, one aches, toting testy prosthetics on Protestant bones
through humid halls hung high, lined with bottle-lensed crones.
Titian's *Venus*, please, among walls of monotonal moral drones.
No Bauhaus, surely; but *en flagrante*, Goya's florid, fleshy tones.

MAUD AND LUCIEN

When willful Maud led poor, compliant Lucien
eight steps under to Georges's unearthly mausoleum

one can but wonder what her Frenchman thought in
throe of copulation beside a dead child's coffin.

Did he consider madnesses of grieving mothers
on the cool slab floor while he dove and rose by hers?

One imagines whiskers dragging at Maud's mouth
in December air, its dryness her heart's own drouth.

Did he embrace the spiritual, mystical mess
with Yeats's neurotic mistress in half undress

his beauteous Irish thespian's desperate dare
politic pater dutifully traipsing anywhere

no protest risen in that modest Samois cemetery
resurrecting a boy she could never bear to bury?

Dubious regarding rousing mobility in the dead
black trousers, black shoes; black skirt above her head?

No matter. Mending her magnificent hair, buckling belts
Iseult's conveyance felt, he'd well played the Tarot dealt

and piously praised God, Maud's belly plumply swollen
he'd not go shinnying up again from awful requiems stolen.

Pretty Head

Just call me angel of the morning…
— Chip Taylor

Lavender on mauve, their languid excess
numbs drawn sinews of thinning legs.
Tested, less dexterous in love than when
tight-gripped we tarnished the lustre brightly
high on a vast brass bed's lustful mattress
clutched hands nearly holding
                                         breathlessly, we
lose again your pretty head, its scarlet mouth.

How could I? I no longer know you, but know
still the rhythms of your heaving, know
the hours of the clock when you turn, dream
wake. I know the doors you leave
unlocked, glass in sink
                            rumpled
socks by a dressing stand, and know these
are not our lives, what then was planned.

Scatterings of mortgages, investments
land, tuitions should chance ever fail us. Once
this child's age, less staid, more bounce
than any feathered flounce of the Opera Ballet
we danced, too.
                     Serenely rocked decades
weathered, seeing you nod recalls splayed
strands of blonde hair on foreign beaches laid.

VIEWINGS

i

Seurat of mind, her tongue in cheek pointillism
applied with practiced alacrity, precisely approximate
admired by plotted paces apart — a world or so —
renders abstractly in sloping, prismatic gallery glow
where only detached viewing reveals no schism.
Closer to the spot, parallel prestidigitation colours both
articulate bots bereft, left alone, two blots of hearts.

ii

Better they'd dared nothings so avant-garde from the start
gutted as they were, scarred by their desecration of fine art.

By Le Danton in Low Light

Long, long past, and long since he'd seen
$$\text{suddenly}$$
in glass, passing Le Danton the quick glint refracted.

Between rendezvous rushed, catching her at table
brushed-back blonde tumbled over green eyes.

At twilight, in that false spring out of season,
she protested, *My leaving is no treason...*

then fled histrionically, lost to horrors of reprise.
Little surprise
$$\text{none wondered at their demise.}$$

QUAI DE TOURNELLE

He had come to the surface facing down the stream.
— Ambrose Bierce

Our thirsts unquenched
the long nights clinched seared her bed
until, unrehearsed

               hair-tearing
warring churned and bled
corpses in shreds.

French Catholic hierarchies
class and social norms
she did not relent.

(Fin...)

     Fin!

she pled, unblocking
torrents of tears.

In a quick, impolitic turn
of events, she fled in stockings.
Thus, he learned.

Wearisome even in fairest guise
wisdom wears a thin disguise.

Rain in Venice

...they tell themselves that tomorrow
will bring yesterday once more.
                        — Pico Iyer

Gilt gauze, dim light mirrored through still air
prisms off glistening marble floors, striated beams
dust motes suspended, impatient leather heel-toe
ticks, the light steps falling, the plush light leather
of Venetian sandals across cool, marble floors
heel-toe heel-toe under tapers flicking
behind thick doors, tourists crossing marble floors
floating thick as fat black flies above
black boats thick in stinking canals.
                        Who unthinking
foresaw so many nattering across Saint Mark's
susurrus and shouting through its cool square
pigeons floating, flying at squinting, scarlet-faced
punters hunting who they'd never twice wed
legions upon legions, hunters in the tumid air.

Near the twilit hour, *a lume spento*
burnt wicks pinched, so many devoured
diminished by long lines, no charging lions leaping
but stained and still on once lustrous plinths
their landings by narrow boats going hence
water taxis racing away under fine mist.
                        Shabby
glorious city teeteriing under the weight of whom pays
your way, does he remember, does she remember
where they are, who they believed themselves to be
when once they spied and paused to watch William Hurt
at Cipriani's Bar plying tittering girls with Bellinis?

Fine trip! Arrivederci! Ciao! Ciao!

                        Deck to deck
funnel faithful tourists before Medicis
genuflecting.

So long! We'll see you soon!
Arrivederci! Soon! Soon!
      thrown down from every railing.

Before January's fog and flood sailing, casting
away from a stinking city bought with blood and
bones of merchant saints entombed between damp walls
in narrow stalls selling gloves, boots, porcelain masks
their sellers think, prevailing, *Ora, vaffanculo!*
        Vaffanculo!

Savouring bloated boardings and, more, *les embarquements*
they go, waving at their drifting off to traders in other ports
facades less lifted, grieving their floated, sinking
         shop-worn
     wreck.

Flat On Île de la Cité

Of Sainte Chapelle, one would claim its light
as a scintilla of God's, but small in fraught
frightful fragility — *lumière rayonnante*
bliss-blazing its primaeval, all-effacing
equity easing each tourist's rapturous flight.

Yet there are graver rays than His
terrifying in rarer, purer beauty.
O do not move
do not speak, only
deign idolatrous fidelity.

She goes from here as the dawning swells
when the hard slight hags and the bronze bells
clap tongues and ring
                              resounding outright
rising from retreating, clandestine night.

Lutetia's priestess-icon, no faith to prove
weaves, drifts not unlike a dandelion seed
released to the Seine's luffing breeze
under high green lamps, which throw halos
over loitering idlers, the boozy, pimpled mugs
night-owls, roustabouts, rookie thugs
lazy flocks of fag-end leper-beggars
who graze edges of sidewalks below a flat
on Île de la Cité.
                       In seasonal, resplendent
catwalk morning, a patient, recurrent ritual
unfolds with the usual crowd has come to know
she goes, practiced in self-pleasure, stylishly
designed, her very striding each step just so
abiding the buskers and the bums
is too cruel a thing, is too unkind.

Secular Cantata

At night, alone, I marry the bed.
          — Anne Sexton

i

Remember, say you remember

                       remember
when they claimed what none could
ignore, a pair wears each other
arm through arm under
lucent Corsican sun, charm of moon, slumber.

Dilations of eyes, balmed mouths wide
coarse sea salt, exultations of assumed rightness
all that is now
as unrecoverable as the lie.
                   Dante
traced arcs, un-demarcations at dune's edge
and rose and fell with Adriatic tides voicing
such choruses, chants to all whom were lovers
gay and young, who made explicit coupling noises
quavering, illicit poses among toppled gods
who would not abide it
                       human myth made epic.

Unfazed by temples blazing, remains of immoral reign
they walk under murmurings of wounded and dead
dimmed eyes no longer dazed, and there scan
vast plains by war's weariness won
oiled bodies carted off in Louis Vuitton.

ii

He sleeps among crumbled days as if among stone
blocks fallen, cast off from Marciano above the beach
while sea waves wash over marble lintels leading
to bedrooms above a garden by seaweed overgrown.

Their song a thousand chorales
                              while the wind
stumbles, yawns, then whisks unclean
corners of memory's ruined city, plodding
wraith-ghouls going from a dirty place
through dirty streets. Playing
like a hand of Brahms
                              it leaps
the desultory wind sings, murmurous
You have become a thing none can see.

What species, then, is the beast?
                              We know only this
(we know). He heeds to a genus keeping
razors underfoot, forever skating, spiraling
down in concentric rings constricting
towards unbearable heat.

iii

Sing, she sings, sings to gods and to man's glories
on a broad, flat Mediterranean strand.
Beside the Sicilian sea, about her throat, she carries
beaten discs of dark bronze, sacred orbs
of Sciacca above high, armoured breasts
bronzed light breaking clouds.

Covering her eyes, she sees
                              a mother
who wears the former's fragrance, walks
her daughter through chestnuts, talks
as if a wind through leaves at dusk, in rain
on the gleaming streets of Saint-Germain
below its precious *église*.
                              There, taking
three *cierges béni et censé*
for him, for the pair, their spectral selves
in the ancient, sacred glow

                          hers
by a dozen others. Knelt, she sees
a white sun float like a Laconian ghost
risen to lift her into air
home to Rue des Beaux Arts.
                          There, musky, sweet
Vêpres, prayers, pungent, treacly-sweet
                                        lustily sweet
amid scents of Chanel *parfum*, fill her head,
which holds his crease in their Olympian bed.

She pages through notes kept among guarded things —
photographs, letters, historic forms — each stinging
breath bearing toxic, ancient vapours
vacant repetitions that do not escape her, bringing
the withered goddess's flaccid vans
to this infirm wings lacking volition.

iv

Dark and dark, a deep, enduring dark
marks their slow end.
                          Shifting, she
switches, turns to Radio Classique's rare
Rostropovich, his fraught, rosined bow
amending their ever-ending adagio
mourned by a disconsolate Russian cello.

Because it is my heart…

                          As if in memoriam,
summer comes, then blows off again. She pauses
labouring to taste heat and citrus zest
her sitient tongue doing its best to savour
lemon and bitters essence, sensing instead
sudden, subtle tweaks of iodine, a litmus test
from that fatal week in Avoriaz
                                        leaving
flavours of fresh blood on snow.

Two

Priest

Doloroso; rather, *žalostný*. Languishing beneath drapes of water oaks
decommissioned men repine, vine cuttings, smoke rising in ropes
spectres scanning shreds of discarded *Fakt*. In their worn cloaks
ex espios decode ciphers, rumours, stub-end exchanges brokered.

Three swans cross, black-banded, waddling trodden banks
three turns take, the lissome Vs plane through undulant reeds
against the Vltava. By the point of Strelecky Ostrov, bent priest
black-banded, crosses Charles Bridge crossing himself and thanks

no one for his nothing, *nic*, save a penitence approaching farce
unreal works not unlike those of shirtless men by eddies turgid, dark
water stinking, obstreperous drunks double-crossed by blissful sin
bent-necked, lice-bitten under soot-barked trees in a beery park.

(Pretty virgin, cygnet waif, transmundane jeune fille with Mercier's face
Opéra loft far, not Prague's diesel-choked streets, filthy trams crying
tourists, arcades, Żubr bars
                            but resplendent Vendôme, Chopin dying
chasuble lost, paps pendent.
                    O repent not our rapturous, malefic grace.)

MISSA DE BEATA VIRGINIE : GLORIA

Cap by cap, jangling jolly
                            caps and bells
jesters juggle green and gold balls, jingling
flute and bell joyous at Christmastime.
Decked in reds and greens, happy the harlequin
consort plucks Josquin beneath acid-eroded
gargoyles while, surging, splurge the tourists
petit enfants and-balloon-men swelling
a pretty *place* to merry claps of Emannuel tolling.

           Din-din-don!
             Din-din-don!
               Sonnez les matines!

Fuming Jaguars, Jags and jewels, static
traffic hums in roseate morning on Rue du Faubourg
Saint-Honoré over-packed with spangled revelers
melon-breasted women toting branded bags teeming
sacrosanct and weighted with Christmas tithes beaming
tree lights, tinsel, and Hermès rags.
                        Urgent in spending
unrepentant at Place Vendôme, on Rue Cambon
crimson and green boutiques ringed with chiming
ornamented cordoned doors swish open and shut
to regal, transcendent entrance notes and tones
tinted-glass U-boats unloading *les vielle Catho dames*
SocGen's merry, monied crones.
                        Abruptly, *les belles*
fall in, privileged Parisian Überclass, to pampered charge
towards the sempiternal siege of Chaumet and Boucheron
disordered queues ranging a final blanket barage
gorging brimful red stockings on Van Cleef & Arpels.

Banke Hovedet Mod Væggen

La misma noche que bace blanquear los mismos árboles.
Nosotros, los de entonces, ya no somos los mismos.
— Pablo Neruda

i

Cotton-tongued, of blight and blitz
unremembered ways, blade cuts
quick, clean, in neat surgical lines.

I, too, had over-prepared events.

Three taxis then a grey and black Citroën
Jounals, plays, screen rags, dated photography.
Years lost in Madrid, tearful if contrived.

Taking leave, she concluded none survived.
and retreated to bed, sleeping the next day.

ii

One o'clock, three o'clock
                five —
sighs, yawns — none mistake her eyes
for sparking stars. (She opts for sadly wise.)
Circling systems collide, decline, rise;
twirl about each other then fuse
fairground rides flying, she apprises
shouts of visceral, kinetic thrill, a touch obtuse.

It is dizzyingly true, and at once not
this pedestrian spin, a forgotten exhilaration
fists clinched tight with bliss, hard and hot
beneath a fluttering bedroom fan
a final flourish, a finishing
kiss then
              the meta-dramatic exit and kill.

iii

Carnivorous appetites drive us thus
mortal conceits preclude us, she suggests.

He recalls her endless preparatory fuss
that none broke her stare, holding
each instant as she did. *Time claimed the plans
we once avowed, then disavowed...*
                              She posted
notes from monastic years in Thailand.

Under such high, unchained clouds as those
unendurable remembrances suggested
how much of her remained untested.

She tracks her thoughts, gazing resolutely.
Fiery nebulae by the Tannhauser Gat
Prometheus kicking against a convoluted fate
at last unbound, and film's eternal child
                                   orbiting
round and round, round in its vacuum
towards immaculate, cinematic grace.

iv

Drawn down, deepest hours give up
a human detritus of wasted powers
still lives through Hopper window shades
emptiness, remembrances of clichés
dropping off a sidewalk's edge, chased
by waters purged from open hydrants
over eroded shards of Portuguese ceramic tile
from floors painted with faded Art Deco flowers.
She calls the waiter, reminded of a lover's smile.

v

Two cats shriek in feral hiss
by a neighbor's garden party ending;
Rude, pissing cats having a claw-and-barb go.
                              Declining
days of softening delight
his steeled spine bends, weakened
vertebrae failing to stiffen

at her departing long, far, foreign,
starting their un-ness, fragile oneness
                                        ajar.

Dimly lit in yet another bistro siege
toss-off tumblings of streaming flute
through tobacco air with scatterings of less
sharp pieces of shattered safety glass
unexpected psychological hail pinging
the protective, plexi-sheet shattering
in his Saint-Jean-Cap-Ferrat rental car.

vi

Taking that remotest shore, all but out of reach
waves with moonbeams darting
                                she stayed in
Saint-Germain's gay lights in the gayest city
blotting out each gilt, tangential, constelled ray.
Farthest at their closest, a recurrent
wash of sea foam reaches her, cool, recurrent spray
blown across her arms, as was his way
touching her, delicately, as familiar love will teach.

Huddled tourists seek an arc du ciel luminence
leaning against the lock-proofed fence
stock Pont des Arts photographic scene
restored, imploring westwards of Notre Dame
to stop the rain, but autumn's early chill, dense
dismaying scuds of opaque greys
over puddled, glistening quais sends
them east to a bar near the Grand Palais.

Famously, the chestnut trees wither beige
muddied pools circle a street hawk's stage
his accordion covered, and fill
gutters leapt by insistent hundreds
of Gallic faithful utterly unphased
canted downward facing winter's dread
as ever they have done and ever will.

Medieval bells ring in a colourless église
sing out for the fashionably stellar pair
clasped snugly each to each, passing
ancient towers through the wedding's unease
fast footsteps, wet faces merry, pleased
under their failing French umbrella.

No soul moves to cross the drizzled square
towards the shelter of its vestry's care
open, waiting in hopeful, medieval disrepair
chiseled into a diminutive cathedral's memory.

vii

Hard heels click through January gloom
beneath a curtained, open window
where a solitary man in a silent, unlit room
smokes, his cigarette alight, locating him
then the shadow figure hurries off.
                                    Quick.
Shunning the ochre halos of hazy lights
as if surveilling, or someone chasing
covertly dipping into an adjacent alley
conspiratorial under a stair, running
from shrouded horror

                              a horror starting
with yawning ennui, Existentialist film fare
skulking silently about the scene, two seers
morose, impotent in their fearful rage, thrashing
for surcease of neurotic rumination above
trash bins and police sirens, then the figure

                                              vanishes
out a back lane when, fresh rain lashing
a woman screams, but this time with pleasure
nothing in the script altogether what it seems.

Curtains close in the dark flat; the wind
                                          groans
obliterating the impregnability of night.

He doses his dream's details over apéritifs
but cannot say what they mean in his grief.

viii

There's no easy track to a life, he says, repeating
I mean, everyone walks a hard road;
never a simple way to play such a tune.

Does it count out in 5/4? 9/8? 9/16?
What rhythm section can keep tight to lines
of late-phase Trane, lithe and leaping
lightening striking everywhere, nowhere, low
as river's edge, between Napoleonic bridges
to the green lamps above Quai de Montebello.

A brooding larghetto drives his afternoon
and hers, too, as it once had driven the twilit
gloaming in a 20th arrondissement mood
where together in granite all sleep alone.

ix

He leans into the pale red laminate
counter with broad, coarse, hatted men
from Le Havre's docks, orders
two Pernods and pores over lunch.
Suffused with the loud, local stammer
clattering round us, his words fell
in the rhythm of a sculptor's hammer.

Father's father mined salt outside Kraków;
his father rode with calvary at the front;
mine escaped, was caught, but later fled
through a Resistance shunt, half dead.
He learned the vines and the land
in Burgundy; a step in any direction
and the soil is never twice the same.
I remember his blunt hands, like claws.
By then, he had changed his name.
The only son, I read law at the Sorbonne
He was embarrassed, but we all wear masks.
Now, it makes no difference how things get done.
In San Sebastián, there's a pretty Basque girl;
I'm leaving Paris; send any mail.

Visions of faces, echoes of voices sink below
the roiling surge of the brown Seine, beating
cadences of brown barges meeting on a slow
brown river churning round curved quais
bound for further chaos, fleeing
charge and blow of the city's
wailing world turning
in its ineluctable
heartbroken
way.

Interlude

i

She awaits her Kir at Opéra
conjuring them from thin air.
                                       Attending
Equus before reading the play, her
mistake, hurredly they scan programs.
Cursorily, but sure, she feels certain all
worship secret, surly gods, drinking
sweat and salt from glistening, blister-
hot cheeks only to gouge out their eyes
blinding each when each has seen
too much of us and only later supplicate them
returning to the plinth to forget
after we've had them, when our very
zealousness for blood-letting rites
the searing pagan fires are left smoldering
supplanted by postmodern archetypes
perfunctory second-life celebrations
which fail to invest art, money, ourselves
with meaning until we go narrowed by regret
without scope or perspective, living
instead our fact-on-fact profit-taking ways
chanting in punch-clock cadences
common to assembly workers or the soft
Prozac rhythm of cubicle-bound, horn-
rimmed sets whose Kahnemann
deconstructed models of best modes by
which highest advantage may be taken
from variances in currency values
stocks, properties, et cetera
in different places at the same time. We
consume, lay waste to lush paradise, iron-jawed
locusts on the wing and for hire.

ii

Starkly, he thinks, *Desire…*
but in his distraction tallies SkyMiles

vouchers, boarding passes —
Cincinnati, Seattle, Chicago the Butcher —
during the forced, boozy intermission.

Posh, blue lightening tongues remark
important things, self-satisfied stars streaking
heavenwards, electronic monetary
men of informed, eclectic musings, turning
seawards, eclectic thoughts burning
good in the mezzanine's comforting care, yearning
in silent, cindery unblinking for the sojourn
coming, Portofino and next season's yachting.

iii

Leaving the theatre, she senses
an inwards centripetal crush
as if into a collapsing white dwarf thrust
energy spent, into blackness, tense
in a choke of traffic, and the dense
dark heat, which never relents.

They believe in one another's faith
perhaps, perceiving little more than glints
in green and grey eyes, singularities
flying homewards towards their little heresies
circling in parallel universes, opposing
forces on collision course into glowing
incomprehensible impossibilities.
                              Compressed
in her conceptual space-time, she apprises
knowing they must inexorably disintegrate
exploding in some unforeseen, unforeseeable
sorrow, some tomorrow of atoms spewed
from ashen, frozen suns out of critical spin
losing their cosmic luck.

iv

In darkness, his mind's tailings arc
across a gated Parisian garden

over their farthest horizon
vanishing beyond the mark
of conscious or even
sensory apprehension
into voids of chaos's declensions.

v.

In a perfectly refurbished flat
deconstructing the visit of her louche lover
she wonders whether her husband will recover
sufficient mass given everything she isn't.

THE PRAGMATIST

La *nourrice*, sharp at eight at a red gate
unlocks a garden, jangles a bell, launches
into day without a thought, songs from a Clio
round and around rolling in aural shells
pops of radioed import in conflated cosmologies
affirmations of a girl's abstruse ontology.

Bébé in Maman's clutch, from upper window
spies, glittering in early sun, *le diamant*
dans le nez de sa très jolie nourrice
and a small gold loop piercing her tummy.
Toutes mes copines me font ça, c'est nouveau!

Blonde boy wades into blue plastic pool
Georges arriving from graduate school.
Too tall for himself by half, he stoops,
kisses the boy's keeper for whom the child is
no subtle hint. Cool, committed pragmatist
she practices what radically empirical strategems
advancing short and long lists territorial.

Emphatic with les enfants, yet they remain
cloyingly spoiled despite strictest drilling.
Throughout trainings, comic obfuscations
left her all but weeping over the last unwilling
from whom she offered Maman one-of-three
deliberations: *dejeuner, dinner, dormir*. She,
aware of such stupifying chance, takes martinis
or sherry, in the salon at evensong sharing
an occasional Henriot Brut with her nourrice.

Bien sur, there are the usual, visual clues.
La nourrice stands just below a man's eyes
hers, luminous in truest cornflower blue
reframed by a head of wheat-blond hair
comme le blé, which flies below a trim waste
lissome and fit when she and children play.

She bathes, she towels
                        she clothes them
never breaking into Maman's juridical scowl.

In low, snug jeans, sleeveless black blouse
fuzzy slippers applied — *mes lapins* —
the look seldom changes in a routine of yogic
precision, patterns of broom, mop, turnings
of pots, counting cakes for tiny, urgent hands.

Broad-shouldered, petite-breasted, a skier's build
knee destroyed on a black slope at Avoriaz
strong of heart, she has scheduled yet another
season filling upcoming vacation.
                        Thus, free will
and way unfold while the last completes
his wash and all have had settling bedtime treats
Maman uncocks a red garden gate and entreats
with paper-bursts of briefcase to greet her parade.

La nourrice, *chatelaine*, dons coat, *bizes* for all.
On the morrow, she will recover humid, chaotic beds
feed dozy *enfants terribles, enfants gâtés*
l'automne commencé.
                        Still later she will bail
stunned Georges from La Sorbonne, failed
by his daguerreotypes as he assails history's citadel.
No academic, he nuzzles the pale and rare erotic girl
puzzling over what pares off Île Saint Louis.

Painting pretty toes
                        la nourrice nurtures mystery
spare mechanic of future matriarchal mastery.

Plaza de Toros de Sevilla

Sequins, gilded jacquard and guiltless linens
traje de luces of a thriller tempting
death's ne plus ultra, wrist-twitcher
whose muleta's celebration, water-drenched
with sand-weighted edge
attends, begs the hand to signal evasions
the beastly ritual's murderous bets hedged.

Daredevil none deign deny, unattainably light
asserting the animal right of nada's damn-all by
sword-plunge said, no word risen to pledge
each gesture an impersonation plied
off your competitor-predecessor's slashing
brutal ballet. How you dance
                              dearly, only not to die
not-now-not-today; otherwise, why when
when no one gives a happy damn about anything
but swirling self-perpetuation unfurling
faithless tracing of the next hide-close curling
duplicitous passes tracked by some third golden eye
mortal lies and black flies following
vermillion flowers skyward in theie fly
spiraling to your plaza's hoof-trampled floor
roses hurled with a hundred scarlet bouquets
then further arcing, claret flowers soaring
metaphors for sweet years slaughtered
along curves of blocked and splintered corrida doors
you preen, rocked back from your very cause
artful aficionado of barbarous applause.

Here, in a super-heated, vainglorious vortex
sweating blood on a dry Andalusian wind
splendourous against side of stinking Iberian bull
gored neck dropped by mounted picadors
its feint, punch, lunge
                              a blind, sanguine charge
the thrice the scalding rush, then lull
and sightless charge rageing, thrusting

trusting curve and point of horn
at a cost of not less than your straight spine's
cold nerve
            no glory but the shill and you think
the one thought of the one cord-cut
coming, waiting it out, baiting the thrust
good, clean nada galloping towards you
running through its steaming shame
in carmine dusk's savage rising, the blood-
red dust of a nada so swell the heat of summer
murmurs your name to nada until
decent, pretty nada lusts and bends
you back with her tender nothing for no one
bleeding claret-coloured out
into the roaring corrida's
sweet, rust-brown
killing nada hell.

GLOUCESTER BEACH

Come luie with mee and be my loue
And we will all the pleasures proue...
>   — Christopher Marlowe

Rock in ancient mounds surrounds beige Gloucester beach.
(One wonders whether any can envision such a scene.)
Narrow, glittering flank of sand stretched to farthest reach
flatulent sea-bulls ranked, near-naked, each by each, obscene
floundering in broiled repose, smug in snug, imprinted niche
rubbed and basted with fragrant, summery screens
proffer impromptu gutturals Darwinians perfunctorily teach.
EVOLUTION OF THE HUMAN BEAST: WHAT MIGHT HAVE BEEN.

O I dare not critique the lethargic flipper's reach
towards its equally oleaginous sea-cow queen
so pink she seems a luxuriant, over-ripe peach.
One would never stoop to be so rudimentary, so mean
but, verily, she grows more blubberous than a bloody leech.

Tide's parade recedes; yet, impossible to squeeze between
I grunt and go. Discretion is valour, late Lutherans preach.

His Tragic Daughter

A man, she knew, could get from his daughter a peculiar
kind of hurt — one of the cruelest that flesh is heir to.
— Willa Cather

Dare not claim what's best borne unsaid, slow fed
insinuating, chary as fog. Tenebrous, static spectre
during supper or creeping towards knotted conjugal bed
she'll not sleep again tonight.
                                        Boy waits to see her
slip blithely into ethereal air, naïvely unprepared
for marriage's insidious despair; instead
                                        der Vater's indigo
daughter caulks a bath, stains old frames in disrepair
mends their garden with shears spare father bought her.

Were Boy to reach that blue square he'll never enter
touch her round and perfect mouth, both would founder
become sea flotsam by pitiless sea winds driven under.

Who'll not utter what must be owned, as clearly read
as a Tarot deck, feckless hearts facing rending come or go
ever envision it, like white sheets on which one's bled.
Hounding the scent of her, tunneling covers under
cotton gown, she wakes not from benumbed slumber.

Following his Electra-on-the-Brink, Boy finds no safe place
beyond her blazing eyes, and thinks humankind's race
should abandon its chase, discomfited by an acrobatic pair
wrapped unforced about other's arabesques, their
gripping at the edge of night, but it is not so.
                                        Leveraging
what's left, an intuitive gesture, the slant smile of dulled guile
pretending in endless, silent mania, are patterns unplanned.
Poor Boy manifests Cyrano nosing speech-scraps he styles
while livid Daddy roars his alarming, ad hoc discourse
his shell-shocked trooper's battle scars grown vividly worse.

Thus they linger, each attending surrender, each divorce
Pater, Pet, Boy, all false in a filial faith discreetly perverse.

ADONIS AND THE WILD BOAR

Rare, ruined, once-ravishing rose, renounced beauty
announces overlong abuse, foregone glamour
promising no further fullness, bell-weathered bounty
browning in a withered garden corner, mon amour.

Such is ours, love, this deflowering cruelty
which claims more heart, more life than is lent us to give.
So slight, our piffling profit for duty, for fealty
no matter truths or portents sayer sooths contrive.

What promise prosecutes as unwavering as the promise
future seasons pledged by spring's duplicitous giver?
Such lustful prettiness is lethal, as the end of each prom is
for vainglorious captain and virginal maiden, no hither
beyond finitude for either. All tomorrows always Adonis
goes anon, bartered to Persephone's sempiternal nether.

Of Iolanthe's Banishment

By what lapse do keen men not catch such a warning
mantle of unsustainable weight settling, eclipse
obscuring, unfolded pall across a lover's claret lips
whose aching, arching grimace, gorged with mourning
all watch, no recourse but to witlessly suborning
fate's perjury?
>   Unwieldy misery in infinite ellipse
swung, pendulous noose slung an instant before it slips
over murderer's throat, runs jury hastily adjourning
straw-polled, each rushing to proclaim
>   *Queen's needs must!*
In Queen we trust!
>   Resigned, he walks in solitude as a bride
prowls and preens in rags taking sustenance from broth, crust
howling, haggard, protruding ribs seven and six a side.
Mad in riot he prays, baying, and barks all foul men to dust
but in all-suffusing quiet no pardon is relayed
>   no Queen allied.

CYGNET

Lithe swan in green current by Lavenham town, where
goes your rare God? Where when here by the fen
careening water wears devastated churchyards bare?
Imperious bird lilting by your lake, frivolous men
gloat they've found high standing ground in fleeting gain
seek fullness in slight little nothings won
but sink under merest weight of pannae by flight's strain
floated on a shallow, down-fringed pond.
                                        Pretty one
on scimitar swing of balletic wing, why dare rise
nigh out of sight overtaxing cataractic human eyes?
Such bright raiments while sun descends in brief repose?
Do you not spy the puny shadow of your earthly size?

Yet preening cygnet through emphatic summer rows.
Foreordained Leda following her fanatic lover plies.

Secret Longing of the Hawthorn Tree

Somber under thunder in summer's umbrous roiling
urgent low squall, heat of imminent, seething boil, see
red-blushed the hawthorn tree writhe, groan, shake out
long, luxuriant hair torn, rended in uncoiling.
Hear her hiss and moan tempting sullied cloud, spoiling
shameless for the wanton, violent kiss of her lout
the mounting tumid wind churning, lustful leaves thrilled
which cannot soothe theie ache, green on bark embroiling.
Body, limbs effervesce, fervent for chasteness foiling
thrust deep to ground until her lungs but scarcely breathe
gasp scarlet lips such a thirst salacious roots upheave
no serous drop to waste.
                         For whom splits before recoiling
joyous come the vast virginal stain, voluptuous, glistening.
Even cumulonimbus shy coyly off in disdain of listening.

SONNET, INTERRUPTED

Of a word, none in weeks. Believes he's blown
doubts his own presence. Done, there is a furor
his reflection missing from shop and salon mirror.
In courting song, once pining piteous by the phone
colleagues claim he'll not survive now she's flown.
Bloody thing never rings, silence his singular terror
certain there transpires no calling error.
It's her flagrant negligence he can't condone.
Room by room, finding himself the disassembled one
wave by chaotic wave, he becomes standard bearer
for quixotic hearts, drowning hardly exotic, nor fairer
being spared. (Better, he rethinks, to sink like a stone.)

[It was not amusing
 her being thus, ambivalently
 strict yet malleable.
 Crossing Boul Mich
 towards Luxembourg, suddenly
 invisible
 accusing, window by
 window, importunately
 vague yet pointedly risible
 he wonders how such a thing
 awaited, he all ways violated
 each move fated, then sits interminably
 before Lex Aeturna, solo at table…]

Who claimed he'd take and give measure for measure
maimed by pleasure, wears a shame as pale as cuttlebone.

Flat-Bottomed Boat

Not mead, nor stair
     far
fast waterways
    surge clear
scheme's fair end hardly near.

Nor we, dear, wend past death's weir
and love's but a dream, I fear.

Late Along

Screw-turned, shrew-eyed we nod
clock bell hour unswerving
owl-light gloaming, unnerving.

Dogged
       to the transom
late along our dither
no gladsome gonging
sounds to hail us.

Now, hither...

We'll not again start
in oft' repeated custom
when March speeds the thawing
and coursing aquamarine river sings.

Leaving, the cormorants wing
crows caw, darting, and smokefall flies.

Quick.
       Our hard parting smarts the eyes.

And After, Wild Strawberries

for Freddo

By our love, the divine may be reached and held;
by our thinking, never.
          — The Cloud of Unknowing (Persian, 14th c.)

Dreamt, then I brought you whole baskets of letters
from my local greengrocer, fresh-plucked unheard

intending a clearer truth less absurd, refined delights
white Alba truffles, as it were, at Christmastime.

Came fare from ancient mongers stacked along the quais
delivered near evenfall by boys sporting scarves

black bicycles racing from docks round the way
cartons arriving well wrapped in Sunday's papers.

A tall one twitched the bell in glowing afternoon
and I tipped the urchin porting seven boxes packed

high. precarious, who urgently turned to pedal back
over cobbled streets as I took my luscious lingual lot

and spread it on the kitchen's scarred, scalloped block
proud as Punch, poised at the ready; but there I stopped.

For rose not a breath, nor utterance of sound however
long I pulled, pressed, or tugged integrants together

or squeezed and pushed them into odd, strange shapes
best suited to dialectics among diametric apes.

Palettes of divine dark morels, leeks, fresh chestnuts
luscious figs and camembert, two ripe golden pears

plump nouns, ellipses, fiddleheaded question marks…
but found only aoristic verbs to spice my market arts.

It mattered not how diced, laid, rearranged
were form and flavour; I lost the very taste of voice

to sputtering quaver, chewed consonant noise
crockery collections spilling guttural sibilants

reduced yet further by a reheated scorch of silence
simmering, genie of smoke ethereal before my eyes.

Left with only longing on that chopping board splayed
scalded, dazed, realizing how poorly contrived was I

to be heard, in flew queer trimmings to my simmering pot
chef without apron caught, no tricks up sleeves, seized

with a con man's naive belief, speech cleft from nerve
indelicately I shook what should have been deftly stirred.

Late, I served marrow on heart. Your startled tongue whirred
a thrum of sharp words ladled by wings of hummingbirds.

DAMAGE

So, to the end of something.
                              We watched them
fling photographs from his Renzo Piano window
spotted koi in the reflecting pool below
their bureau in Paris. Abruptly
                              he was nowhere.
She then fled with him.

Aghast, Human Resources put it down to
indulgent, self-annihilating whim.

In retrospection, tracing the ghosts
of that improbable, improper pair
how remote and rare it feels
such reckless middle-aged abandon.

Their daring makes one reel
so light, so torrid, a zeal abhorrent
as careless as currents of air.
One wonders at the damage
this ecstatic infantilism yielded
near them
                 (ourselves).

After, none spoke of a man
ravaged by such beauty.
                              Savage
how her looks could kill...

Yet lives level off
                 and many
months lapsed while we considered
their bevel, its evident, resultant bliss
measured against our tristesse against restive
mistrust. From a distance in late afternoon
arises reluctant envy
                              with bled-out thrill.

The Plovers

Where once splayed lovers
braids writ runes on bare sea dunes.

Rare prints of plovers.

NOBODYS

Slide-ways upwards charting, ever over-rife
(if thin as a Christmas carving knife)
greatness gratuitous imparting, sky-shot
rockets hottest everyone's everything's
soaring status inculcated by the fickle
mechanical apparatus of highest repute
in a tailored Giorgio Armani suit
hyper-inflated in an algorithmic age
who never sates but degenerates us
reduces by tons concocted lives
hard won of meaningless miscellany
his itch like hives of self-mocking jackal cycles
a rating jockey's multi-media
Flatus Américaine.

          On the other hand
to best be fancy-fated, glory
consecrated, consider an alternate
lifestyle plan.

Try romancing at home
             go out undone.
Resist, don't be antsy. Clearly alone
never master ballroom dancing, nor
sculpt, paint, scribe, and never sing
today's most famous chance
oblivion's the trending bling.
             Run
to win no hip Olympic sport, flag unfurling
neither javelin, surely, nor Scandi curling
no synchronous swimming flea
rather, celebrate as the one perfect spastic.

Retreat to green grottos Cambodian,
pledge as placid Zen monastic
(a desperate final resort, agreed).
Assume no art at which you please
nor invest your soul in any critic's fantastic

hyperbole; even Banksy's mortally spun
chiseled to death giving capitalist head.
For an edge, kneel in prayer; thankless, become
a nunnery's immoral, excommunicated nun.

O they're out there, you know
wherever they've overtly
elected not to go; there
then here, too, believe me
whatever they forever project never to do
in remote remove from pixilated light
neglected on foreign desert dunes.

Understated, effacing women and
deferential men of purest obscure
weirdly mysterious assassins of pun
in places hardly destined for fun.
                        Shamelessly
fat, slow as they can sprint
cue-ball bald, neither tits nor wits
in shocking secret fits
on anonymous-eponymous display
wielding no celebrity sway
packing not an ab, a peck
or an envied online bun.

You and I, say
two things vacant, eviscerate
no trending curves to extrapolate
nothing anyone might swerve
to denigrate.
             Just us smugly
weathering away inviolate
mere Smiths and Millicents
delighted to stay
clandestine — *obviously* —
neither famous nor gay
aimlessly brilliant
friendless but resilient

cast off by all the spot-lit snottys
our own dwarf stars precipitous
in grotty, glad, mellifluous decay
wildly, always mildly funny
depressingly sunny
not a care for the money
nothing at all in play
unnoticeably scintillant
only yesterday.

Ourselves in a word!
(Or haven't you heard?)
Duly we newly unnoted
no ones, emptiness-inured
neither cooly nor cruelly
truly unruly
          no fools, assuredly

but nobodys.

You Are Here

Arctics from attics, photogravure plates
Metropole's gates, unretouched, un-
restored, one-of-ten-thousand-men
                              running
wool-suited legs long, relentless
bent, elbows splayed
                        akimbo
chase angled disarray
under grey fedoras
beige spilling beige
Burberrys twirling clacking
silver-and-green turnstiles
                              spitting
abstracted Thurber men, endless
                              queuing
trafficked back to urgent suburban
meanwhiles
                line-switched
dragged hacking by glistening
piston-barrels
                    pummeling
glass-kissed
                    tunneling
narrows
            plundering
forge-spun
rubber-lunged
pump-pressed
steam-hissing
rail-crushing
rat-pissing
spike-pulling
steel-wheeling
                    swaying

air-braking
            slowing, waiting
swirling winter out
on a braying hell of a
black & white city's
pitiless iron metal
                  EL train
going.

THREE

Torch Song

Hope Cemetry, Worcester

Gyre-loves soar, furtive E, sums by Fibonnaci scored
yet I aspire to more, and with sharp specificity.
There lives no language to explore it, how we adore
you. Verily, the sly neotenous in timid literacy

during that inexorable march towards sottish rest
none could parse. Like good scotch, all savour despair
from whom dressed and scrived with surgical flair
spilling not a drop behind her architectural desk.

Do you wring water from Lota's straight black hair
or marvel, still, at Sammy's iridescent blue eyes,
brighter blues than Wellfleet's quill-blue skies?
What of fustian Cal, who so thrilled your gay heart?

Were all of these yours or merely fine art?
Tell me, how does one quit the Keys for Samambaia?
Do you breathe better now, returned to tumid air?
Honestly, such mysteries are practically Mayan.

Anti-confessor, anything but digressional
who enounced overmuch in all you dared not share
by stoic word, I genuflect before this hypogeal throne
petitioning an unapologetic pro, both alone

as exposed to light as high-hung moon in white sun's ray
silent, psychological smile your way. (Our modest way...)
Kitten, untranscendental avatar, tell-all inversion
of the tabloid fad, my guileless conversion

is complete; I defer, *surrender*, to surreptitious precision.
Hush-hush stroke of genius by whisky-and-water smitten
why bother, in a jungle, with an umpteenth revision?
Brazilian jaguar at jugular feeding, I bleed and purr, bitten.

BLOOMSBURY MORNING

Life is a dream. 'Tis waking that kills us.
— Virginia Woolf

Tea, first, then weighted stones for pockets
remove rings, bangles, Vivienne's silver locket.

Into our wide, wild chalk stream shall I stride
enough of rehearsed aesthetes, the facile; I must go.
You shall be my art's final verse, Vi; thus, we'll go.

'Tis my full freedom comes, not another blow
but from broad oars drawing back to shore.
In river's languid care, snaking like Medusa's hair
slithering green grasses coil about my wrists
willowy ankles washed low in clear, careless flow.

O let me savour this sympathetic wave I ride —
No urgent, pretty thing born of woman abides —
So ends the endless gossip, now and evermore —

Yes, drop…

No longer my affair, to a clean, cold slaughter
well I know, not Giotto nor any mother's daughter.
Stopped there, shallow men shall claim of my despair
that fashion's awful current caught her
but I shan't balk

            for it was not so.
Let them talk.

(Now walk, walk…

        go.)

Diane at the Tate

And not look away from unrelenting stillness
manifest in every print, the not-understanding
"confirmed in unreality."
                              Not to look away
from the half-invented humanscape, the void
le must never to be avoided. Not compassion
honestly, but a type of competition
running its course, the necessary evil
you said, the frozen pose of one to be shot
pride of shame, blameless, beatific in fame.

Not to look off from the giant Jew
and circus twins, or grinning clowns
with Down syndrome so flawlessly maimed
they couldn't have imagined the colourless tint
of their shootist's shady heart, fashion-quick
poseur so grotesquely framed even the dead
declaim your prying, prodding art, the shock
on both sides of the lens becoming
spikes in a pulsing polygraph.

A coy prompt at opportune time thrills
down walls and the queer folk fall.
(Smiles, they're positively murderous.)
Camera clicks another kill, its work
slick, still. It's merely a matter of what's said
when, no?
              Well, no.
                            No pervy Nemerov can claim
otherwise than by denial, rude film roll
developed for an academic laugh tooled by whom
suffered ridiculous and strict old school.
Too many negatives to look and then not look
away. Retrospectives in galleries like this
truths perfectly unsaid, what was the point?

Such delicious dread, but not to look away
when you have become less saint-like, undone

by darkroom fixatives, sad life exposed
in trays of toxic chemicals, the glancing back
snapped into endless receding, shameful
poet's word-trap transmuted, shifted
towards an artist's blameless inversion of light.

You were your own louring weather
wearing trademark t-shirt and black leather
not a faultless plan. You were your true oeuvre
the agony sumptuous, those open wrists
impossible to stitch together all the dark years since.

Examining that broken, predatory heart
no one could be so presumptuous as this
to blink us apart.
                    Biographer-critics
zoom their foci too tight, seeking culpability.
Instead, I think we now agree on what you were
dying for us to see.
                    And we see, Diane.
At last we see.
                    Always
see.

WHEN BACH'S ALGORITHMIC HANDS

When Bach's trick, algorithmic hands prefigured Brandenburg
he could not have foreseen lowing, lingering Berlin skies
in grey eyes, nor did crystalline trills in Gould's legato runs
those final, murmuring thrills, explicate your German clarity.

That your disconcerting vision should catch me unaware
startled me. From torpid strains in attenuated air
choked with traffic after morning showers, arose a close stray
spill of gilt, of high Baroque in breaking sun. I suddenly woke

the car filled with your gifted polymath. I cannot say how or where
you plucked my key, opened the door; only that you pulled silver
and tortoise through platinum hair. Leaning in, I thought you spoke
from the red leather seat beside me, noticing damp-cooled *Gásse*
steam rising, hints of woodsmoke, leaf-burnt lifting in October.
Twice turning — I reached to touch you, *touché* — it was over.

Dans L'Atelier Selinger

What archetypes are these
insentient man would seize
thus? What mythic hammer
what courtyard clammer
renders formless unto form
in shapes of no known norm?
Through what fictive lens would homo
sapiens sapiens spy himself?
                              Why
old Schlomo's tap-tap-tapping
his kerubs all a-napping
revealed in bronze, stone, wood!

(How little all had understood.)

We?

        Neotonies plunged each by each
upwards, *ses enfants* adoring
from famed, fecund Grecian pallets.
Chiseled stone in slivers
flung like Olympian sons
so soars Schlomo, the winged one
before us wielding
Thor's mighty, magic mallet.

Henry Darger

Sometimes, all you need is permission to feel.
— Olivia Laing

And no one clocked it
kink-clever, your perverse gore
lone star.

(Wink-wink...the shock.)

Who still seeks godly hearts rocked
by atrocities of war?

SOLANAS'S 15 MINUTES

The lost parts, too, are felt to be lonely.
　　　　　　　　— Melanie Klein

Pretty, and shrewd; milk-skinned and tall, they.
I grind rude scraps, my might's bitter ration.
Sola, indeed, for I alone am terrifying. Nothing
flow-pressed through fad's factory, I am Revelations
made sensational.

　　　　　　　　(No melancholy Marilyn, I'd say.)

Hardly one for center stage, literarily
　　　　　　　　　　　　　　relegated
to margins of pages, biographers' footnotes
annotated, a minor character in a pleasant
forgettable play, I feed on fame's spare wages.

His candy-assed blondes pose, dote
in endless ego-inflation. Mine's the price
paid to know, but not concede, one's station.
Inevitability, as will soon enough be known
by whom pixie-voiced patriarchy is overthrown.

Behind his desk mopes mop-headed
Andy, silkscreen-deep.

Dear, call the cops...

　　　　　　BLAM!

　　　　　　BANG!

Fabricated fops
all creeps and queers.

Bleed like me!
　　　　　　(How's that for a crescendo?)

All good machinist girls need a manifesto.

St. Thomas Beckett Churchyard

No one howls...
  — Jane Kenyon

Among our luxuries harried go blue mothers. (You saved my bacon.)
I'd come to believe we thrive but in grief, neglected, forsaken.

Through cool, killing, colossal rage — over-shared Daddy issues
toilets clogged, babes in training, betrayal's damp and draining tissues —

indignant Fury in hair-tearing harpy tirades shrieked her voice.
Practically comatose, I, too, lost all reason, any sense of equipoise

simmering through the noise of supper-time at a porcelain stove
sunk in sinks rude with misogyny's rubble, that fathomless trove.

Sharper than any man might stop to aim, between the eyes, as it were
you touched the spot, my brain hot, reframed by loss in rapturous blur.

Too soon, bubble burst into shards of thrilling verse, you lost the plot.
Cunning-clever, yet it was a crushing blow, Smith-girl ego or not.

Minor poet, one clod claimed — *blamed* — writ in dense testosterone
admitting greatness only as a sloppy fit for an Australopathic bone.

Stung by weary, self-aware tears, death resolved little for us, du und ich.
One thinks of lungs maimed by gas and grease. (*Tch-tch*, they did the trick).

Lotus of the Upanishads, over vanished headstones our children plundering
I stand here knowing there was no purpose to it, pointless, pondering

no sadder satire insists than an adulterer-satyr, half man, hooves cloven
fain with desire, feasting on that frozen fire snuffed in a flameless oven.

O Ariel, under English rain I weep not for your spare, Norman parish grave
but seethe praise to the recalcitrant bitch below, for she was no man's slave.

The Puerile Lover

Compagna devota fino all'estremo sacrifizio

Amedeo falls —

but where is Death in Modi's
Woman with Blue Eyes?

Shrewd Jeanne, all stone-hued moons

                              wise

saw he'd never do alone.

FARFALLA FLOWN

Automatic antennae
taught-guyed
                    metal
rooftops green-grey
                        mottled
brown-bricked
chimney top
bottle top
green and postered
                        kiosk
down-bent Borsalino
brim tight-clinched
American listing, looking
to wan foreign faces
                        sidewalk
tables, sidewalk
chaises, sidewalk
loudspeaker in air
black heaters under
                        blaring
Rogers-Astaire, switched
eclectic aesthetic, Te Kanawa
static-spitting
                    electric.

Farfalla
        farfalla pretty
where in the world will you go
quit from this dismal December city
strange farfalla so
fragile, so
            tangential

        O
                                O
            O

farfalla flitting, farfalla

                    flown.

Lettres D'Amour

Corner-turned page apprises morning by ribbons
laid in languid lengths of a woman's pillow-braided hair
withered in heat, hung hot-quiet, and to the clocks confess.

And vellum leaves, faint fades of sepia sun, doors ajar
to drops of dry August wash, and flights of curtain lace
swaying in ochre strokes of gouache by wisteria's tress.

Metro-bound, desk-bound, by the world hounded, flung
arms, legs unwound in mundane domestic chase
coral-lipped flutterings, afternoon's disheveled duress.

Out-folded ornamental verses noiselessly read, sparely sung
Strauss's fatal late lieder passionately, posthumously sung
the lush soprano and, richer than this, each evening child's caress.

Twilit, day-long eyes, and rose-tipped in listlessness stirring
yet they yearn, and the dogs sleep, and the cat purrs, and seized
with grace, lovers unlaced, pleased in breathless undress.

La Feuilleraie

Il y a assurément un autre monde,
mais il est dans celui-ci...
            — Paul Éluard

Saintly, plump, three self-aware swans slide past white herons
while the Cooper's Hawk glides upriver by Boar's Head House

where five black cormorants dive for orange-bellied bream.
White-faced owl last week, then a startled new chouette

clear-air-drunk on juvenile wing, slipped twice down the flue.
Embarrassed, there she glared, clawing the mantle, entreating

what she demands from a tree above the cliff, *How dare you?*
I was not ours to take, she insists. In late August, all balk and

autumn elides quick days, skips along the Seine towards Paris
September's frigid fingers tickling bare napes of bronzed necks.

High, honking geese chase a linear trace towards lonely moon
re-weaving winter down, which in April all preened to undo.

Who in daft dotage wings away in chafing December? Nor I.
Await bluer days but mark, here, how fast fall's gypsies fly.

Crone in a Paris Metro

Hag, harridan, to no traveler accede; in spleenful sedition keen
vent ruined breeding, villainous virago, shriek out your blessures

bleat no false contrition, none to grieve a heresiarch cur
toxic-lunged, razor-tongued, scandalous in civil treason.

Station to station, pick dirty nails into winter's lesion
nurture iniquity, your sagging face a slag-heap figure.

Rail, rock this subterranean world, snag alien pest, gorge
on gossip and gore, bloat of rancourous, retreating years.

Sovereign bitch, vitriolic victim of perverted princess fiction
defrocked Teresa — *A vous, pétasse! Les gays et les negres!*

Matriarch who sparks the tourists' knife-attack dissociation
apostatic witch, recant the psycho-priest's oily ablution

renig the nag who'd be upstaged. Shrew unrehearsed, *rage back!*
Page by page, unredacted, sift your stack of spinster fishwife rags.

Lara

Plaza Roma, Buenos Aires

Liquid links in rivulets enlace
thread serpentines of shimmering chains
entangle untamed, unchaste girl
guileless in olive stains
chaplets of ochre
                   strings of Argentine
squalls thundering in scudding greys
cloud and fallen sable curls
in a garden under drapes of
                        clinging
broad Ombú leaves becoming
waterspouts streaming
               streaming.

Solo tango in luxuriant, verdant hour
weathering through a walled, wilted place
carmen, erotic, willful pout
                   tilted
on clever, aqueous face
alert, empowered, her
             wry wit
writ wild, explicit
crosses a carnal, engorged
red-luscious
        mouth.

ANGELS ARE

Wanton death wish me unwisest, deranged, dangerous
downsides up, replete empty withouts, withins unmade
tall-most raised above zeniths of secret, insatiable sin
so decadence-damned by impermanence all angels are
us-scaling not-new faces up from all traces of unknowing
outside spaces, native worlds, which availing saner we sang when
tomorrows untamed by you were, untimid in out-glowing
frightful night's fierce forever glittering moon out-showing.

Pledge, betroth no promise after now's all of always, transcend
mere mealy-meaningless meta-words vainglorious chasing
chaste we unbidden unto fulsome hollows, hale bodies begun
quickly thickly honeyed endings scarlet-hot, harlot-volcanous
un-shy lovers uncowed by cool, clean fires fleshly unfasting.

Nor regret nor not stay unlasting, not yet (evers never lasting).

Desert Crossing

Smarted, she craved him clearly
locks laid light across his mouth

yet her darting tongue
                    stung of drouth.

Such Release as This

Hear...
> east wind's kiss brush crisping leaves
in ardent rush, and catch the scent on auburn hair.
Listen, then. Its letting go of murmurous prayer
yellowing among sheaves. (We are not of these.)

Fire-melt pours unto emptiness; how we grieve
for it is not the nature of insatiate need to unbear
us towards lesser quintessences, states beyond care
unshared, but because it is inexorably so, none believe

wild, tempestuous east wind and all she disleaves.
Rare, origami Buddha, who flits but fitfully cushion-aware
gathers great furor to infold a species' hearts in disrepair
transmute our transient lives on your titanic knees.

For all, once.
> For all lost and shan't again receive, who bereaves
such release as this? East wind, seed and husk release in air
but wait, wait, await her fairest flare then swear
and heave high your unsparing heart high as you please.

Heave, heave upwards until the lightness of that shriven heart
rips you, riven, from your seat. Then heedless, friend, start.

None

Matins, vêpres…(but you never speak of compline).
Or that there's no godly reason to grow fig trees
and tomatoes are like words blood-luscious, some green
a few never ripe to eat. The moon, pocked glory
a hurl of dead earth *en reflet*, what, dear Louise
do you mean to say? You opine but rock with sophistry.

Please. I suspect you speak merely to appease
nonsensical metaphysics in absence of the divine.
Behind Apollinaire, our bench peeling at its ease
in a browning park beside a medieval église
surrounded by pieces of cathedral frieze
sublime, you know damn well you can seem to whine.

Scribblers over-conscious of propounding as master
become psychological scriveners sounding disaster.
It pleases, sure, to leave a winner, ego's compulsive disease
prizes recovered from crusts of Pompeian marble
however the archetypes are excoriated, garbled.

Like a loaf of dough one's forgotten to leaven
or gazing into space, which was bound to cost us heaven
rust-edged Irises comprise not an astral throne.
Voices. You hear voices when each is your own.

You know this. You know tickseed are but floral weeds
through which tomcats gallivant sewing tomcat seeds.
Acorns to hawthorns, even golden swathes of corn
signify rien du tout, not a thing. You're forlorn with good
reason despite faith in flowers, pluperfect poetic zing.

Yet, square to bevel, whether some or none of this is true
impossible to love and not to woo, doing everything
one shouldn't — so wise, so noble, too — all levels at you.

Crask Inn at Dusk

nothing which we are to perceive in this world equals
the power of your intense fragility...

        — e.e cummings

Up from Crask between Lairg and Ben Hee
ursine men peel sedge, cut deep bogs, dense
with long-burning peat, while by Scourie
bent women slog to slice seaweed at the stipe
from slick rocks at low tide, then sling green kelp
over lines and across weathered, salt-licked walls
fighting wolf-throated winds off the North Sea.

In coarse, bespoke wool sewn long ago in Sutherland
bearing an iron-black briar brought from the games, I
turn to cliffs, and clouds scudding above Eribol
spying a crooked lass cross low hill and hedge
broad in shearling, a weaver's skirt, and leather boots
hauling baskets of bricks to stack by a stoop
sussing her half-gloved fingers, cracked and blunt
no longer feel the fineness of a needle needed
to mend ragged sleeves pricked by thistle and burr.

In October, they hunt hare and great monarchs
snap necks of plumping grouse and pheasant
the moors cold. London gunners come at present.

On the beach, I kick bits of wood washed, bleached
kindling for the refurbished croft, flat and dim
dusk settling in, and mark scatterings of lights
in leaded windows of villages far and up the edge
of tides towards John O'Groats, then move south
down the Highlands desolate middle track
past Tongue, Ben Loyal, Ben Kilbrack.

In Paris, a man is proposed nothing to lack
unlike this stark place near Hope wedged
between Naver and Shin where only by way
of dispossession does one find true faith.

You learn to hear whisperings, the wind's pledge
chasing wild up ancient glens on sharp gales
cutting Altnaharra with quick, sharp summer hail.

Rambling, I heard a voice, and sensed its breath
warm and moist, touched the suprasternal notch
below her neck, paused to watch the Vagastie
wrapped in moth-mauled cloth from Harris
and poured a flask of Wick's brume-softened malt
to the green thermos of black brew I'd brought.

Briney scotch in an enamel cup, it spread
through me, crack of sun on a steep ledge
rising the way sea trout lift from broken rock
by the loch's sunken manour, seen then unseen
at the carved bank's drop, gusts folding in pages
slags of creased ice waiting, drifting in stages.

When first we sighted Crask through slate-dense
rays of late afternoon light devoured by the cledge
she sat under its bleak tight ceiling, open hearth
scented with ancient burn. We thought it heaven
drank and ate in weighted air, and still I breathe it.
Unbound, it squatted there, and we believed it well
and assumed its ancient spell deep in the dale.

But this — granite-bordered door hewn new
and true, a chimney's tall and burnished flue —
it ought not have been reborn to suit
an age she'd grown to grudge, its tartan floor
no more to trace light steps of ewe-shorn socks
small with chill, the will small, too
after gripping over cool round lichen stone
in the old glen's late afternoon
clambering and hobbling
onto crumbled border fences
fallen into Scottish snow.

Gone, all gone and long since
gone, but the strong pull doesn't stop
with you still here, still so near.

How ever shall I find you hence
without your sodden-footed prints
trod through this sacred earth and sooted air?

By goodly Celtic gods in their heathered lairs
I swear I do not know.

OLD GHILLIE

Lent to run the hounds
sleet on heath, where monarchs bound

by pub hearth found, spent

cups downed —

Sang o' th' Gōd an' Lukky Wer

O the glades of life he felled far forward, meticulously rehearsed
upraising baroque facades with Ultra-Panatar splendour
appraising, *It is thus to live, a good man made never to be cursed.*

Slight as fluff, the stuff of comic opera expressly versed
embodied projection over pristine strand at dusk's translucent hour
that rare staged life he'd far forward tell, repeatedly rehearsed.

Bemused in equipoise he beheld even his tender garden burst
amenably into flower, burgeoning with morning's clement shower
declaring, *'Tis agreeable good, a hand-made man who's never cursed.*

Astute, he most auspiciously wed, disbelieving such fortune at first
plenty added to uxorious love, betrothed with unconcealed ardour
thriving further, faster in all things forward, needlessly rehearsed.

Manour, holdings in countless spheres, grandeur not to be reversed
mounted and he peered at the lot with conspicuous Christian candour
reckoning a pair spared. *Man beckoned unto good sleeps never cursed.*

But when base autumn's sere-frost left that fair fey bride inhearsed
he slaked all thirsts in grief, rebuked arid earth, reviled each honour.
Traitor angels betrayed pride, power, purse while he aimlessly rehearsed
Say my treason! Unmade for no reason go all men, godforsaken, cursed.

SECTION

Four

Kitsch Quartet

i

No Context

Lightweight's heft and haul, heavy promises, half values
the bet lines declined, plane, texture, hue
present in a windowed view, a clutch lowest rung.

Nordic Man, Marlboro Man, Hatted Man unsung
under broad-brimmed cover in dive-and-diner scenes
shady men baiting, illuminated in stuttering green

fluorescences of fake, inexorably we descend
into knowing-not-knowing, flickering
tube-lamp lives unfixed, neither out nor in

richness in desolate spaces, the post-Noir indigo-blue
meta-narrative disconnect, out of true, riding the EL's empty
piped-in beat of blank, cable-strung plains of plentitude.

Where thin, weak muscle rubs against gristled rib exists
no-place-no-witness-no-group-no-blog-no-context-no-nothing
authentic only in its alienation, tongue from tongue.

ii

Brand Promise

Square in every platz, place, *e piazza*
insists no punier fiction persistent
against long throws at lousy odds and bad sense
precarious-resting, preposterous,
uneasy, lache on the endless list of things
the French despise, i.e. that anything,
everything American is possible and
the thought of the striptease she sings
in a world that insistently resists her naïve
you-can-be-anything-crack-a-new-curb-appeal-life

that New York City knack, her unbearable, happy
PR hack into 4-H lightness, her legal crack
beginningless pilgrim possibility riding
horizonless Chisholm Trails sitting parade-
high in a robo-carwashed chrome on pink
drop-top Independence Day Cadillac.

Only, those who live the NOVUS
ORDO SECLORUM taste her towering tripe-
stack, the republic's con, sidewise hope
oppressing every mother's SOB cashed
out for this helluva joke.
                              Hell, boy, not even
khaki G.I. Joes in Saint-Germain round up twice
starting so far back, sorry sod-busters of the boulevard.
This most made up made-in-the-USA myth goes
down hard and deep like long blows of RJR brick
bellows, like Lucky Strike smoke choking the prettiest
perkiest Pollyanna with its black-lung trick.

Sonuvabitch, Jack, not even the lonesomest
cow-pie cowboy crossing the wide Rio Seine singing
his O-Suzanna-ne-pleur-pas-pour-moi comes flush
grabbing a stake in a sow's ear gold-rush.
                              Dammit, Jack
this poorest, proudest Stars-and-Stripes-Forever kid
is the Goddamnedest Redman-spitting, Indian-killing
sun-silhouetted Hollywood ending always westbound
ass-crack-grinning big-as-Texas-lie aimed dead between
every hustling rustler's Rayban-hid all-seeing eye.

iii

Kingdom of Kitsch

In this mist exists the Aesthetic of the Hit.
          — George W.S. Trow

Shite-fisted, or florid with rococo trills,
every click clocks its bit-mined cliché; tin
digits infinitely nimble in their fix for

                                    numbers
climb endless ascending strata.
                            Peach-skinned Jills
and preacher Jimmys locate, define themselves
by rapturous thrill in apt compliance with binary
data-dots exact in each extrapolated psycho-
graphic relay.
                        Bars on catalog backs, codes, lists
torn from a trillion sheets of green-and-white
perforated lists, profile plots in predatory
mitts plot meticulous angles projected to
pixilated planes, every phone jockey's wide-eyed
Why not? terminating in gleeful, gainful
                                            Got 'em!

Word and movement reduce to unreal
stillness, constitute and comprise the construct-
demography where target variables are
calculated, inculcated, collapsed into
bespoke graphs on HD displays.
                            Indefectible
virtual, invitro meta-seeds by media farms scatter
games of thrones paged out in neural yields
while shoppers in shopping malls, vast swaths
of knowns under true blue skies as bland and flat as
Kansas grown to reason for the Christmas run-up
each urge harvested to all-devouring pre-conscious
silos, fields of flowering impulse deals
nursed and cached to seasonal towers.

Here is your new kingdom, Trow
pilfered land of inverted truth
endless expanse of totalitarian
kitsch
            where nothing feels worse
than the algorithmic itch no twitch
can reach, consumers switched
to the whirr no purge can untransfix
bastard bad-boys betrayed
by beatific brides, angelic

evangelical faith known only
through devout doubting, milled teeth
and nails laid pretty while razor-cut
rows are laid flat for the grinding
the recombinant shill ever on go.

So say it to me now, at last.
                              Unwilled
culled from what cold call am I, screen man?
Fast-distilled, my skull's precision-drilled crust
content cast unto tomorrow's markets
shall our hearts not come to doubt, to grief
to rage in the cool, clean hands of your
trust-staged entertainment brand belief
its preening orchestration, its vacant
eviscerated, marrow-and-
brain-swilled leitmotif?

O say it, say it to me; play it for me as white
noise until I can't take it; fake it to me once
again until I am utterly
                              consummated
by your violence, the joy, the mathematical
kiss of our sovereign dollar's empty relief.

iv

ONLINE MEN

*It is no measure of health to be well adjusted
to a profoundly sick society.*
                    — Jiddu Krishnamurti

#OLM/WEB/SPINNING

Angled, insistent, insidious insider
sedulous, web-spinning spider
counter-mnemonic, jagged
                              macerating
hunger-split chelicerae, devour us
unbuild the world by grab

and grind
        by feint of eye
soft-hack-sly, exploding all economic law
feeding the cyber ventriloquist's maw.

Relentless in triturating
toxic teeth eat, deflower
all comers, your very cause.
What appalled mid-century mind does not
feel the bite, the parasitic jaw
cleansing a generation's bones
of a strength that was never theirs, after all.

Out of the way, make way, here
they are, new to pretend
               the Online Men.

#OLM/CAPITAL/PREDATORY/CALL

Direful in hardwired diminishing, lethal
under-awee, these new men of Empire
whose wars yield what long-suborned progeny
grew to abhor, our booming, breeding
acquisitive selves.
            Ephemeral
as fairy light, deft, greedy as sprite elves
flitting from capital to capital, predatory
mocking every ethicist's goodly rationale
no hope in histories revisited.

Columns advance by automatic trade
move into positions plotted, coded
from cubes in high-tensile steel towers
uploaded by geeks and freaks in godless
cathedrals, downward glowering
spires of mirrored glass, each breeding
none safe from the digital power.

Agglomerate in rise and rule, acceding
faceless, nameless, come
               the Online Men.

#LOM/NARCISSUS/GENERATION

A man's man judged — classic, courageous —
self-referential jugglers, juvenile
Jurassic
            guiltless in green-helmeted heads
yet moderate in life, neither bold nor dull
who kept the catacomb wracks sagging full.
It was our time, we winked and pled
soldiers, mathematicians, clinicians, yet
now the days are sick with us, stooped, stopping
traffic, mounting our bus, its harried driver
doubting
            Shall I ever be thus?

How alley urchins glare at us, their faith
felled, scythed, hybrid iterations of unlinked
lives, our Narcissus generation gazing
into pools clear of haze, dust, and clutching
all-seeing, through shallow depths towards
unworkable
            analogic meta-conflations,
unsustainable irrelevance measured and
monitored, nailed to a cross of virtual stations
where the liturgy calls unto
                        the Online Men.

#OLM/MONEY/TONGUE

Distant, studied, they shall come to regard
our appalling decades of late greatness
inventions of improbability, confluences
of impossibilities, a shop-lifted ingenuity
fashioned with a conqueror's conceit
preordained by our very mediocrity.

Claiming we knew no better when
hell-we-knew, entire populations
unable to conceive such a darkness
collapsing in the long, white night

of the capitalist's easy-monied reach
their cordoned private beaches
reduced to glassy melted sand
again, again, again in atomic waves.

Affected compassion in dying light
our arc like a tracer fading
in a jungle fight, we bore
                    the Online Men.

#OLM/CIVILIZED/ORDER

Who can otherwise explain our neurotic
andropause? Does the chasing, shilling
super-machine seek applause?
Do its grinning dead murmur
together of engendered blame, banker
men banking ineluctable shame?
Unrepentant, whose plump, full-fed fingers
play beneath an existential roulette table
pushing the planet's Patek doomsday clock
towards its final, nihilistic tick.
We, who thereby forfeited civilized order
unthinking in our profit-taking
can but look ahead, furtive
abhorrent, to
            the Online Men.

#OLM/MERCHANT/VAMPIRE

In our time
            the self slipped, shifted
from industry to art-form, to commodity.
Who is not a celebrity in these empty days?
And switched again towards
self as meme, an animated thing
onscreen
            instantly forgettable
Instagram and Facebook scenes.

It is the question of our age, a bar game
accommodated to cocktail hours
after-office in dour public-houses
or following Sunday's monuments tour
a look, a clue to galvanic, glad-
unlearning daughters and sons of profit-
vampires after bloodied slaughter
a closing query, a cue
tossed to fellow entombed
who yet pursue the knowing
                                        deceit
the affluence of regret, our debt
called in by
                the Online Men.

#OLM/GLOBAL/GRIMACE

At the end of now, the cowed men
the wowed men hem and haw
while financial news hawks
their great trompe l'oeil
genuine lies spreading
apace, cutting tucks from
an accelerated global grimace.
Few fathomed fully the heart's economy
read its algorithms, as cryptic as Hànzì
a binary plan driving the postmodern hunch
our barely borne hunger for on/off
human touch.
                    Exposed in misery, this
dismal place secure in devolutionary mystery
we stagger at the scope, the cost of wow
the very hopelessness of hope now.

Who lost all repine, congratulatory
of the misapprehension in our
                                vacuous gravity
our hollow hubris, superciliousness
comforted us as sacred crusade, causeless

in our collective depravity, the prideful
unconcern, but we would not see it
releasing virulent new strains
of pretension as corporate-funded programs
whose cynical pop-priests and
                              sub rosa
pogroms ceaselessly churn to expiate
our sins, and in that hologrammatic death
begin our black star demise,
                              the avatar rise
of *di virtù* men, vile, voracious
sentient things no god would devise, foraging
ever encouraging the gorging of
                              the Online Men.

A Czech in Vegas

Thwarted strategems. Instead one looks to urgent surgeries
months, years hence, scourged for a life of immaterial perjuries

awaits the smashing hit of morphine in the single, mobile hip
then diminishing melt of celestial drip

precipitous tumble down the rabbit hole of anesthesia
a base jumper's rush and luxurious, forestalling aphasia.

Soothed, like bits of ancient mosaic smoothed by the Ohře
where once we cast for greyling in dry August, luck spotty.

Who hopes the lost days to be understood by progeny?
It is naiveté. They seek the least taxing patrimony

remembering childhood duplicities, the eldest most of all.
One would leave them less deprived, less mean and small.

Fine and true friends…let's be honest. Five? Three? Two?
Who'll come when the needle pricks, little left to misconstrue?

Inane in regret, hollowed out by loss and its perplexity
one lives one's debts, decrepit men with limited dexterity.

You, my *zlatíčko*, your innate Cartesian bent served us well
until that final hour at Christmastime, our seasonal hell.

Nafplion and sisters, you wrung spotted hands, thinking *America…*
Off plan, precarious reasoning failed even Eroica.

I've read they found a city mislaid. Many gods; no belief.
A remarkable state, raised on high ground beyond churchly grief.

Their king erected houses of plenty, none in need, no relief.
All loved, lived in joy. His reign was predictably brief.

Not Smith, the Scot, but Lenin, cunning bastard, was dead clever;
closed his fists, tugged the Western gallows' triggered lever.

So I remain here with showgirls, gambling, and weather
wondering if we might see you again.

Ne, I think. *Ne, ne,* never.

GULF STATION

Grandfathers, fathers, veterans victorious, many
and mine returned to us, glorious men in *Gas*
small at siphons on black-tarred back roads, tractors
pulling tack where no car, bus, or semi passed.

Aerial map marketed, seven days awake
waiting out the fated station
flat grit and grease heaven's own
three-dimensional invitation

not to worry with tenant-cropped piedmont
where its overworked and unrestored tobacco-
bowed trucks rust, mud-caked folk art disintegrating
sooty as a Venetian museum's attic-find Rococo.

Unstudied, unwistful, lean beyond
comprehension with man's unfulfillment
relic, anecdote, black and white memory
yet in certainty striding fallow fields, family

counting greater than Boston Consulting's
calculated allegories and stupefying projections.
Wrenches turning, he claimed, *The false poet
travels...* So Big Papa derided, knowing, then jacked

another carburetor, cracked hands and black nails
requiring no guide, no prefiguring, no purposeless pride.
When business fatally dried, he retired to his loose
porch rocking through Scottish mist back to Caithness

leaning against a low croft's fieldstone walls
willful, unblinking man whose round head
strict, plotting, worked the tall, humming red
pumps where Metropole's glutting engines fed.

Up Green Country

for Tris

Heed by hint in dusk-light caught
>feral-ribbed
slinking under an R4, ravenous cat
slots through the fenced garden's benches
soft-padding over fractured paving stones
and chiseled sills of Saint-Julien-le-Pauvre.
Cursèd cat, black cat back to its slatted box nurses
blind *chatons* behind the Hôtel de Ville.

Now-and-then coming, then not
a quick, curt note from a pal
saying late winter he'd stay in spring
forgetting what was planned, stinging
enough forgotten.
>Pacing through
an hour's remembrances tracked
from smutty windows over the brown Seine
clearly seeing what once we were.
>Then broad, flat water
mirror beneath cloudless, high blue-sky
clodhopper county jon-boating
broad, cold Fontana, Brent Santanya
guiding a low hung, wind-beaten way
towards Hazel, Forney, and Abrams in May
light breeze pushing the bow
in early Appalachian summer
and the boy's blonde hair blown sorting
hand-worked wets from dries in that high
dangerous hillbilly range up strange
grand green country,
>the last good country.

On the Veldt

[I]t is a profound consolation…looking for meanings,
only to see in the eyes of others of its kind that it must die.

— Peter Matthiessen

We cut our teeth trailing shallow, hollow prints
on shadowed snow where Kilimanjaro glints

sloped steep and grand above a vast and arid veldt
hawking the crags, tracking that rarest spotted pelt.

Masai jogged their great expanse of sere-scorched plains
walked flats in tall straight lines hunting abortive rains

where chiding hyena with tormented lion fought
for gazelle those ferocious chivvied blondes had caught.

Canvas tents staked and guyed, four men at the watch
we cooked prideful kills, thrice poured fine malt scotch

then seethed at dark-stashed beasts barking each name
unable to stomach their rotten, dung-stinking claim.

Mark the stalking, twee-tongued savage stood upright
talking blood, bred of pitch, pristine, primaeval night.

Come With Keener Eyes

Once I moved about like the wind. Now I
Surrender to you and that is all.
                                    — Geronimo

They will come with keener eyes, far finer men
casting clean, farther out from our reckless din
who'll not bow down to all we ken
phenomena of our violent, vanishing vision.

Spaces between galaxies are not greater than
this; silences between notes are not so quiet.
Succeeding the last, before the next instant is
no longer than the lapse, boy from man.

Ours wear antique watches on harder wrists
write to their sons with sharper pens, cast flies we tied
with rods we built; ream pipes we stoked, then rest
prized spools on mantles or in beaten desks.

Few further hours to plot, nor to correct their letters
nor spy for them red-spotted browns in green waters
on the Risle, the Irati, le Doubs by Besançon
where they sign with truer gestures once our own

who in their new world will give a good goddamn
pause, turn, clock current and rise? How far, then
now so near, watching braver pilgrims retrace our drifts
wading quick, strong runs we could never ken?

Moon Man

for Armstrong (1930 – 2012)

Muscled bone and gristle, yet a life deathless
in clouds, breath and blood by flame forced.
Ozone-owned, in crazed ice clothed
comet tails swept the sandy blonde hair.
Infinite gaze blue-eyed towards suns, moons
Saturn missiles, heart's thrumming chambers
gunned when, thunder-voiced, their chorus roared
clear, sheer will heavenward boring.
Arc-backed, earth's boundless curved horizon
who highest tore astounded, speechless men unto vying
once when young and sky-found, flying
                                        astral

soaring —

ON BROADWAY

Boot-Men on the beat pound
scorched, unpeopled streets
cheat by slant of word, peal chants

War Is Peace!
                    clutch
rifles, bibles, hoard their cash.

Cold cant rumbles, cuts like sleet
needles slinging at bubbled windows
steamed with deep mid-winter's

greedy call for further dead.

Voiceless husbands and wives
sickedened mothers, friends, lovers
undress, deep-dive into sleep's sweet
quiet while bold the drums quicken.

Unroll the flags
                    light the candles.
Sleep, sleep through all appalled tomorrows
sleep turned to the wall, and weep.

Borne back, she rides home alone
on six brass handles
                    via video feed.

SERIALIST

Say you pull it off. Charm the lot, scam whole clinics of your
boorish shrinks, puffed-up charlatans. They grieved; none twigged.
Yearning bodies caked in disbelief pack your crawl space, adore
coroners retrieving uncovered ribs, skulls sidewise jigged
for a scalpel's scraping, the DNA still pure.
Obfuscation the fact of facts, your fatal game rigged
cat-and-mouse toying with life, death; auteurist scourge
any port in a storm, *n'est-ce pas?* All promises reneged.

Your thing's the play, our cries the score.

(Fast, fine, the saw howls…)

We swooned, thrilling cliché killing us. Podcasts rattle
with it still. Kisses soliciting, your pudgy scowl
elicited when we grew dull, fattened pigs, debased chattel
approaching the basement abattoir, we were slaughtered
cheek by jowl in secret rickety racket.
No regrets, yet hedge all bets, fiend
                        lest yet you forget
how meanly bags of bones will prattle.

Sacré Bethléem

news from America

Bethlehem, beyond Atlanta. A mother
murders four children. Three, then another.

Pillows fluffed, she plops upon the face of each
suffocates all, believing their breach

unbirths immaculate, the Will of God.
Neighbors are fond of her. *Good with kids, if odd.*

Green thumbs, her fresh-turned sod
spared not a one; she relentlessly spoiled the rod

calling those lambs to fall proud, to reach
high the Lord's Kingdom (a farther Myrtle Beach).

Papa once drove her with Momma's brothers
his Ford blister-hot; she thought she'd smother.

Nor did she hide the pregnancies. Why bother?
Even dead, they looked just like Sissy's father.

ELECTRA, BABY

for HMN

...united at last in a father complex so apparent that Dick
winced for all psychologists at the vicious sentimentality.
　　　　　　　　　　　　　— F. Scott Fitzgerald

i

She burst in shrieking
cursed, blouse cross-buttoned, stinking
of sex and a night of drinking.

ii

> Hey fiddle fiddle
> little ditzy diddled
> piddled by father
> heart in perilous bother
> none so fancy the riddle
> glad fingers leave written
> across cleaved, creamy curves
> of dozy, dreamy moon
> the least he deserves
> thinking,
> *You've learned so soon*
> *pretty puss purring such a tune*
> *I'll have you whole, kitten*
> *without a spoon."*

iii

When Daddy crept late
into the black room where she slept
swept back flaxen sheets
groomed her bottom
she hardly demurred, bed-ridden
but more than this, she leapt
to devour new power
over mama, tragically less wanton.

I orgasmed as a girl,
                    she reveals
to puerile, smitten lovers
but there is much in her squealing
they never discover
a pleasure so complete
she fears nothing under cover
drawn to secrets of her incestuous lover
when she knew she had got him.

Three brothers, two cousins, she
schools the lot of them until
urinary tract, renal, bladder
surgeries retool her.
She does not recover.

Years after, unchaste decades raging
in backswept introspection
alone she dreams, half asleep
of interjections yet to discover
murmuring, moaning
                    Daddy
Oh, Daddy…
                    sad waste for truer others.

Beatrice

Pump and thrumming, steel drums hum under blistered fans
green-gold dolphins breaking against crusted blue walls.
Beattie's husked voice conjures blood across the low, lush island.

Batista yet to fall, the take from the warm, clear Gulf fine
fast, fat, and clean in sintering heat, Papa glorying
storied cobia, barracuda, flash-quick and arcing marlin
sailfish flying, the white sun blinding.
                                Sugar-brown and thin
gamy Cuban women, hard rum and cut cane flame spitting
pink *langostinos* thick as a roller's wrists.
                                Clubs jumping
the bar spills out salt-sweet daiquiris while you play Whist
at stained linen tables until four then drag buckets
filled with ice and Perrier-Jouët to the beach,
                                    insistent, humping
in aching morning drowning in fine, bleached sand.

Fidel's decades, decay accured,
                        El Floridita shimmers out of reach
memories interleaved, grand palms above the devasted strand.
Stifling nights in the Keys, catching Gleason's breezy band
you watch bubble machines, radiant dancers, swaying wraiths
mislaid in Habana's wistful scrim, its translucent, thinning haze
that glam romance of days,
                  phenomenological sleight of hand.

Bird Time

Not everyone wants this conventional little life you're
rowing your boat towards. I like my river of fire.
— Zadie Smith

Hiss-hot hip-hop in scarlet sizzling she says
she-can-she-will in the junk-time-all-night-
Bird-time end-of-millennium cop-you-anything time
too-dark-for-the-Brits-time hop-hipped
through sweat-choked Gitanes air in black arcs
dense and shadowed in bet-your-tight-ass-I-can-
time under Gare de l'Est eyes hit-hollow de Chirico
streets dark-and-deep-and-dead as shadows between
hard dark thighs wide-spread and pretty as a needle
steep and stark as smack-debt in Paris June's
velveteen dead time money-green and grinning-
mean in the hiss-hot ache of needle-thin summer.

Bingeing bad on big-bottomed bop, players
drums stopped, golden horn dropped in naked wonder.

6 Octobre

I could never talk to you.
The tongue stuck in my jaw.
        — Sylvia Plath

Witless emptiness explodes across discomfiting cosmos.
Whither, mon amour?
                Bully gods in ecclesiastical spasm
cosmologists bungle across bascule-bridged chasms.
Bombastic Nostradamuses born of clinical temerity
wrapped in baggy blue hazmat suits unlock hidden parts
reveal cardiac ganglia in hubristic half starts
but precisely nothing impart. Approximate fine art
no Big Bang cause for broken hearts, Eros's dart
rockets aimlessly in endless arcs. *Geliebte*, heart's mystery
decades on, you spark and sizzle comet-like in contracted veins
synchronous something alive in a disarticulated brain.
Synapses gone dark yet strive, fire through our celestial history
where cruel, covetous Henry stood down your stout German will.
Glad to ungrieving sod this day, hard bastard,
                        a lover's belated kill.

Murder in the Gym

Hetta

Full bar open, their secrets
brokered, a slant phrase quick-turned
Forget me, she pleads.

If not now...? Lips part, the wind
speaks. *Breathe out, in; breathe, breathe again.*

Adam

It's slight strain to spot
her pleasure in my hearts' thrill
though she pretends not.
Shoeless, so soon to the dance
still she wills us; how she flirts.

Hetta & Adam

The most impossible things
we keep of gay, golden days...

In an endless ache
the thousand cuts and bruise-stings
insufferable, unspoken.

Hetta & Suzanne

We were each other's
perhaps too keen to be had.

Studied, gowned ghosts
full-blooded, willful lasses
by plodding, clod-footed lads.

Adam & Mitchie

She was ill-prepared
for December in its end.
The lavender dress
in an earlier fashion

the stark whiteness of my hair.

Hetta's Gang

LinkedIn friends, bound by fine threads
frayed, fragile, none so agile
without the others

At life's knife-edge there each sees
each towards a gymnasium's gaping breach.

Hetta's Measured Exit

Come in faith, go thrice fooled.

In that fated gym, their dated school
plays tired, ancient music
where girls take newly practiced turns
deflated, anacoluthic.

DALE "DENNIS" MARTIN

of Mrs. Phillips' shame

El hombre se muere de frío, no de oscuridad.
— Miguel de Unamuno

Death's in the good-bye.
— Anne Sexton

We loved you.
                    Instead
mad bitch trussed you to a desk
cinched shins and thin wrists

while all bore sickened witness
to a thing too cruel, too sinister displayed
before us but dared not turn away.

O those grievous tears
from that small round head
the wail, which flew from choking lungs.

Twisting, you hung there years after.
Who would not learn rests twice appalled
now calls to retrieve you despite her.

Sudden, serendipitous
dear, so dear to us

how near, your falling laughter.

Le Gitan

for RH

It was never important to live long, bovinely;
but it is essential to live well, divinely.
　　　　　　　— Walter H. Londo, PsyD

In a pinch, not to squander nor squirrel that glad gypsy heart
to sure-seeming cinch, enflamed gambles of the punter's art.

White-hot, the house pulses, pulls players but wage-smart
sweat-marked, stark not-maybe victims claimed by dark

save you with that wild, willful gypsy heart for your wonders
thrill us ever by rarest beat of life, beamed light, who blunders

never stood nor lingered long with griefs of reason. Bandits
moneylenders, usurers, and otherwise puny pundits

paramours, thimbleriggers, dissembled ratfinks
deck counters in gold-lamé and diamond-glass cufflinks

calling in the devil's every debt, what gangster disbelieves
strong enough never to slip polished cards up sleeves

or off slick bottoms of a slack shuffle? Say whose
mesmerist truth suffices truly, and why to cheating ruse

we wager weary selves on soul-snuffing plays of not-a-chance-in-
hell at canted tables to fiddled, elliptical odds of roulette spin?

No bankable end is long served fumbling big-wadded bad bets
towards a swiveled swindler's swell of the false god's get

neither yours nor mine when there's little try to tempting tricks
of unholy loss, chip stacks pushed fool-hardy at double-schtick.

Three corner-bent pairs from nimble, tumbling thumbs dart
but don't do it. Stick. Hold hard to the vest.
Go guarded, alert; stay the test.
Glad-blest roll all, loved and loaded, with your luck-sharp gypsy heart.

HARRY'S POST BLONDIE

Harry's paneled New York Bar
serves American hotdogs
with French's yellow mustard.

Blondie's came hard straight-up
mostly clean, hot in the bun
heaving with relish.

Fully fallow, I go all the way
kraut and sweet, thick mayonnaise
nothing in between.

O glorious days of diner dining
pink fetish franks fleshly cased and steamed
decadent delicacies, as if a dream.

Now I claim our seats solo —
Harry playing elite Sunday polo —
morose but faminshed in peckish pining.

Strung up at Harry's door
how I keen, hankering for Blondie's
bountiful, bottom-heavy leaven.

Nothing I need more
she'd gleam, a dog between her teeth
which briefly explains the bore

I've become in umpteen
grades of mean, penitence from heaven
greedy, rotten through with green.

ON THE LAM

Lo, thine eyes dead-lift
red lids, wry by grift

                     short shrift

times lean on the lam.

Split in two, lean, suited man
cry it true, "I am!"

            (I am...)

True Gen Redux

Say, pal, that one thing you swear you know
and, boastful crowing, here declare it so.

Listen, this is the true gen redux.
Damn all to hell, there's no good luck.

Work for it. Take it.
                    Play
it out. Live it.
            Write it true.
                    Then
shut up and — Basta! —
                    make it new.

Le Bon Américain

Ihre Sicherheit ist nur durch ihre Drummheit möglich.
— Franz Kafka

Bison slaughter
Cherokee and Apache
killer, nation thief

woman hater, witch
burner, slave trader, railroad
builder, land grabber

cattle rustler, gold
digger, snake passer, tongue
talker, faith healer

money merchant, loan
shark, arms maker, war peddler
flame thrower, fighter

jet flier, napalm
dropper, atom breaker, strip
miner, sea dredger, river

diverter, water
poisoner, cop on the make
union buster, migrant

blocker, pledge taker
petroleum man, plastics
man, big pharma man

crop duster, machine
rancher, strip miner, woodland
deforester, coal

burner, dredger, star
gazer, comet chaser, black
hole speculator

pulp printer, blogger
muck raker, podcaster, spook
lyncher, book burner

news faker, polling
station intimidator
vote denier, court

justice shammer, clerk
seducer, Scout perverter
altar boy hustler

gymnast molester
child porn hustler, match fixer
coke cutter, crank cooker

phone tracker, trader
card hacker, market fixer
debt buyer, Okie

evictor, psycho
whisperer, guitless man's
executioner

schoolroom shooter
scalper pusher, tits and ass
lifter, gene splitter

fentanyl seller, mover-
shaker, half-baked man of stone
wood and dirt mason

carpenter, farmer
rabble rough planner
hardscrabble schemer

grave digger, dreamer
pick-pocket politician maker
prayer book in hand
good goddamn
        American.

SECTION FIVE

Menelaus

*J'entends les conques profondes et les clairons
Militaires rythmer le vol des avirons...*
                                    — Paul Valéry

Launced, O Gods, my blade-laden ships
none shall dare recall from war.
Scanning seaward years hence
from this high, far promontory
how shall I mark them come?
On bloodied shields, no further worry?
Thus harmed, would they then hail
a prince, or Helen, Paris's whore?

There's no lesser creature good
for men to abhor than some
conquering monarch's ego-death
carried as the dead's grave worry.
I'll watch overloaded boats leave only
to return in grievous wash of slurry
thrust of wind, wave, and wood
no Olympian can restore.

It is a piteous affliction —
there is no draught, no cure.
Many, so many champions
too many either to save or to inter.
Why now call them back, beseech
them at all? Preordained, out of reach
bones and brains soon laid to bleach
on foreign shores bereft of glory.

Not King!
            Fates, 'tis what fools do.
Who might for me blot out her face?
Wretchèd, I'll catch their rotting race
shouting anon,

            Menelaus! Disgrace!

Collaborateur

Bad men need nothing more to compass their ends,
than that good men should look on and do nothing.
— John Stuart Mill

Leaping *fillettes*, pallid maidens, thirstful Baltic tongues
slip into corners of parched mouths, in and out, hands pulling
cigarettes acrid, stinking in laboured asthmatic lungs.
After, when regretful sleep is all and you feel only lulling

moth-girls thrumming under arcs of summer, hot as a gun
at La Maison, angled bones and blushed Pauillac-kissed cheeks
dun-dusted by nightwing until she's a cut, a gash that runs
up your spine at a corner table, her numbing bliss all you seek.

These charades are merely saying you are dead, too, and were
always dying, and maybe she wants you but not tonight and you miss
everything about her French despair then nothing and the rest a blur
or not a blur but dead clarity knifing through night like a cat's hiss
below an open window above streets where desultory wind insists
you spin out with fellow dead in a gavotte of war's dizzying twists.

Irma Grese

We shall not escape Hell, my passionate
sisters, we shall drink black resin...
> — Marina Tsvetaeva

Torahs torched, lamp shades cut and sewn, you cluck
of Nietzsche, flout in sheer decadence abrupt German will
until your devout shill polishes off a century's madness.
Impossible numbers; you must assume our sadness.

Bayonet-straight spine in an Übermensch cliché
parrot-marching parody, unnamable homicidal thrill
in the skull, audacious as the finale of Stravinsky's Firebird.
Teeth, we wade through seas of teeth, gaslit, screams unheard.

Mengele's kraut-coloured wheel of eyes pinned by the sill
pale and cloudy as steam from the trains, no fate to fulfill
tired of light, wicks drawn down awaiting betrayal
there was nothing for us but to ride your dreadful rail.

We tolerated ash, our unspeakable stench, stupefied
by your implausible, terrible skill.
                              Parasites!
you shrieked at us, who were eaten by lice and mites.
Schnéll, you snarled neither complete nor contrite.

When — *ker-rack!* — the scaffold dropped with a jackboot clack
you swung by a thread of thinnest irony. *Wellkommen, Schwester.*
You're now one with your murderous sisters. *Wir heissen dich.*
Wellkommen! Du bist jetzt einer von uns. Wir haben dich sehr.

Vichy Beauty Queen

pour S-J

O ruthless, perilous, imperious hate…
           — H.D.

Draped in bolts of iron, bold, Wagnerian, aligned
Alsatian shoulders squared to 90 degrees, divine
barbs, your axes exterminate our undead pleas.
Your east and west a taut, surgical line
to your great credit we sussed not a sign
crazy, fateful plot predictable as flights of bees.
Elated? We were euphoric to lose all you came to seize
raving to be caught, to die entwined. (Few could decline.)

Such callous crimes were never wholly yours, of course.
Imputed to genes, latent cowardice runs best on automatic.
Gallous girl, true evil seeks its cures.
Counting corpses? Who wouldn't be ecstatic?
Solingen prick to the spine? *Bien sur*, good habits inure.
No murderess, by God, but a damned fine Vichy Catholic.

Société Nationale des Chemins de Fer

pour Marie

...the lesson of the fearsome, word-and-thought-defying
banality of evil.

— Hannah Arendt

Golden girls wear stars
bear SNCF boxcars.

Locks, curls —

       skullcapped jars...

Eichmann

pour Charlie

Yet what it tears apart for meat
Is merely what its victoms ate.
                    — Djuna Barnes

Hyde desk-bound, whoring Dorian, Drăculea
creamy death-drunk impaler, your deflated corpse
hot-veined again; cool-fleshed freak of simulacra
still-birthed in revisiting, a new pulse drums
in lumbering lupine limbs. Your guilty stitches sing
like electric jolts from a great machine
until vacancy seems a solid thing
glassy as the glacial tears of Frankenstein
composite of lightening and polymath
stitched to wield egregious, eternal wrath.

Here, keep you clear; dare not wake the psychopath
heart. He eats his own and doesn't vomit up the lot.

Piecemeal man, you're fiendish-clever; contrary, odd
but who lusts over-hard, jests at blood, rots in scarlet sod
harlot of merciless gods
                    forever.

COUTANCES

pour Corinne

Stone-stoic stands this self-willed house soon to fill
with sand, vying by heedless seas swept
to beach, which once kept children wild, urgent, free
who slept, dreamt, played small against your hill.

Call a dirge, douse the embers
church yard and stave remember
war's humid graves where maggot, worm
and sly field mouse sate, once mere slaves.

Purged, pleading of that damned, devouring germ
sleep sanguinary kings supine by wry, hapless knaves.

Tache de Naissance

pour PD

Travail, Famille, Patrie…
    — Maréchal Pétain

Fiend, friend — *compère* —
the mark of our century
is its feral, nationalist hunger.
Ravenous, we choke down
obscene obsequies: princes
ministers, presidents; fathers
and sons; priests and gods; swallow
mistresses whole and avenging
wives who once adored us; lose
promise, most sacrosanct of loves
savaged among helices of neurons
ribbons of snapping synapses
packs of clinicians, cynics in bars
the cerebral shunt.
              We exist
beyond belief, faith, hope
like so many emphysematous
breaths whispered into parchment
wisps of heat on institutional air
watching the tunnels for centaurs
who do not speak.
              No absolution
chants below, in cloisters of a ruined place
no grace, no unction for brethren in their
diminished, unrepentant choir.

Friend, fiend — *Capitaliste;* tart
with an ataraxic, calculating eye
it corrupts our age like a cateractic mist
that dark, ensanguined, malignant heart.

March and Dirge of Vichy Dead

pour les avocats

Already the crows are grooming themselves for you and your people.
— Charles Simic

Shambling sullen among them   *les républicains*

you pick up their *mauvaise foi*
dress in their clothes, the Catho

                                        dread

clinging always, then at last

                                        you succumb

days dragging into endless waiting
hopelessly plodding

on. We turn in straw beds

                                        wild-eyed

sleepless in unending surprise
trodding through tumid afternoons

descending unto unforetold nights

                                        hollowed out

sockets fixed on nothing
but our bleached-bone camarades

annihilated
whole, gone to nothingness

                                        néant

while we un-join with all our force,

clinching through horrors of

                                        grieving

death's dissociation
knowing not how or

when we'll fall, ever

                                        ungrounded.

Down and down, downwards

                                        declension

to bleak history banished,
women and men, the village lot

no-excuse-no-blame

            so many

deny their own names.

Only disingenuousness remains
among our indifferent damned

            entreating

fellow fallen spectres retreating

with further scores of revenants

            following

by cart, rail, roundabout
gathered in doubt

crossing

            the turgid Seine.

We slog alone together
without purpose, pass

slaughtered livestock
writers shot, and

            familes of *gitans*

decomposing in ditches, beyond

betrayal, knowing not what we now

            know

know, that there is no avarice
like cowardice.

Sainte-Mère-Église

            despairing

flag-droppers blown from beaches
cathedrals vacant
shattered rail cars

            permanent

our blind choices binding us
to the lie while the scent of shells hang

            in air.

Our wind-up clocks kept
with clacks and tocks of time
who sleep in wagons, in papered boxes,

weep by melancholy priests
stooped and sack-clothed,

du royaume; thus we come

by cow bell and drum, all with death

winter Sunday's marching,

staggered by these clapped-out caissons
no guarded truths showing, best unsaid
gravely, shamely going, all already

Istanbul

Wind-spits and a split of thirteen
crows crosses thirteen trees
shrieking, cawing beaks
                    daemons
black in beseeching, uniformed witches
in acerbic Turkish stitches
                      of lament.
Ancient shutters rattle, crack
against a house trembling
as to the giant's approach
                    stamping
marching, closing,
              dancing
in lunatic glee.

          Under towering
minarets, we wait out the storm.

A chair,
       a book — but nothing moves
in the stillness of the *avlu*.

Next morning, yet
            we follow
slits of dull grey clouds scudding,
caravans lowing towards us,
approaching across a malevolent sky
in the long delayed, impatient pace
of the westward-advancing race
roaring in thunderous chorus:
                    War!
Its comes! War! Just there!
             Warning!
Warning!
       Drums, guns, war... beware.

Ave Atque Vale

Blast not death's blare
                    rear no trumpet
forbear. Lorn battles lostly won
triumphs dearly blundered post costs in blood
good sons claiming but night's rude red moon.

Approach slow, swear fealty, your pity
fair and kind.
                  Dirty pits dredged in vain
war fain waged far from Loch Doon
dove, stoat, fledged hero drowned
bride brooding, kinder rocked

                          each wept true.

O the tear-blotched.
                  None bore well
solemn Verdun's brume-sifted sun.
Who lang slept in this low, bloodied hell
cloaked in mud-clotted weather
never hears the heather-tartaned piper's
pensive, rheum-shrifted tune.

Tumbling, they fell and fell, all here fell
limbs strewn, all fallen dumb all too soon.

WILL

crossing Narva jogi Bridge

Rose lips bleach, flesh rots
where bore-eyed geese-men shot dead
who wept,
        who pled not —

Rose lips bleach, flesh rots
where bore-eyed geese-men shot dead

THE WILD SWANS

for the Albanian women of the Kosovo War

Beat the tympani! Crash brass symbols!
Trmptet their fanfare! Exult!

Heigh-ho!

High-leaping heroes

alive with lightness heaving
dismiss all vain bereaving.

Unloose that strict truss
all false fuss rigid, ruinous.

Wise in right unknowing
the hunter's tense, quick bowing

and hound's feral bark
arrow smashing to great hart's mark

sharp whistlings as of looms weaving
cloth of clouds leaving, leaving

leaving.

Heavens in fiery damasks spin
towards fatal ends; yet, bloodied, ascend.

Approach your zero hour
fallen flower by flower

embark on wings wild with undoom
into soaring comet bloom.

Who once was bred of woman's womb
lilt as do larks among unmarked tombs

unfinding death's prick and sting
undying in some far, starry ring

outside our chaotic world
vans flexed, unfurled.

O moon discreet in nebular heights, reapprise
night's unvexed angels in serene fleet rise.
Sweet seraphs, wild swans of Paradise rise,
                                        arise.

Zero Is the New One

It is easy to be dead.
  — Charles H. Sorley

Enfeebled, meek of speech, stutterers each
wailing evangelicals who seek futile exemption
none are forgiven. Towards your end you reach.

imploring, *Redemption!*
                   Rumour
gossip, I started none of it. The war-
maimed and slaughtered babes, planes

down behind the guns, ships lost at sea
little wonder they've hung the plot on me, I
but a humble journeyman.

The human genus in infinite declension
believes in exception. My council is ever thus:
Speak all things you've never said

                           have your say.

It's a gift to live simply, free. To play! Elsewise
what might any professional man plead?
Deacon, warden, psychopath

life is light, the weight of a child's spelling bee.
Over-invest; you'll not find gay salvation
sprung from mortal seed. Do your best.

Broken-hearted, phlegm-filled lungs
wicked or the good there's no unflinching man
who's not once clung to the flimsiest rot of rung.

Not the proudest punter stood, all go queer
in the throe. No dispensations, the sincerest
wreathed in stems or diadems all became Lear.

Lord, Buddha, a Queen held by so many dear
kith of gods…all were whims, moods of mine.
None the worst, each contrite, every father's son

the simplest math, a numbers game, null set
said and done. No ill will nor maudlin regret
parse the speech as you will

                        zero is the new one.

So bring your brass, spell for a pint; fling
some skirt, flirt for a stay; pray you'll join swell
Mephisto another day, but never forget

                                  there's hell to pay.

Rubbing Tombs

All that came out of them
Came quiet, like the four seasons.
— Chuang Tzu

Teach me to go to a country without
without names and words and terms.
— Thomas Merton

Odd-cocked, of wheeze and bend, December-thin
who no longer intend the withered lie, our nostalgia
for nostalgia cast rearwards with pale, milky eyes
minds socks of fog, we are too late to begin again.

Untethered, yet we will not turn back again
to where we waited, timid and tired, stubborn births
of children whose giddy grins today but half inspire
yellow years retreating from the heart-eating desire.

Bold in ways of war if torn, we descried
gunners lost on green-teeming coasts, shipping seasick
home, hard struck with grandfolk gone to our surprise
each by each we believed we'd grown middling wise.

Beaming, boastful sons batted home winning scores
towards a season's ultimate victory. In proud chorus
we shouted, throats swelled (unhearing the deads' retort).
Renewed, we cheered, crowded the fields of their sport.

Sisters to monasteries in Bhutan, beyond reach
and brothers, gypsy twins to ancient tribes
conjoined, today we scan for relics along a pebbled beach
then remount our bus, Michelin guides in hand.

We cry through the vacancy, beseech and exclaim what was
more literately descried before. Tides running bitter
fear leans close to us grinning, grifting for a faded cause.
Above. we rub chalked tombs lifting illegible letters.

Surly men, stubbled double chins, flesh bound for dust
we settle into small flat seats. Escorted to our hosts, we
mount the V.A. stair risen sharply steeper towards us
the band perfunctorily glad. Defeat is ever thus.

We lose our pockets, fumble keys; piddle done, we thumb
beer-stained pages archiving all the mightiest generation won.
No souls lifted nor gods to gift, alight in this gentle burn
we grudge His going, too, with whom none trudge in return.

Sons o' Northern Clans

Dae nae shanty true love o' dear ould Ulster
for its clough and bawn o' clover is th' English lie
as Scotland's tartan'd skirts bear th' Empire's indigo dye.
Slave, there's nae slave freed ne'er a free-plunkin' busker.

Nae tell ye hail'd from Belfast beaten grand
or lorn Caithness dales 'neath a Highlands sky.
Kings cry out for conquerin', 'tis no finer why
dyin' blooded thru 'neath Celtic banners banned.

Declare instead you'll slave for th' cause.
Dyin', swear rebellion proud in independence
claimin' Celtic ways by way o' Celtic laws.
Nae further pretense afore a false Queen's offense
pledge you'll meet th' breathless dark wi' nowt a pause
bràithrean perished in arms wi' ne'er a sov'reign pence.

There'll nae be any tellin'', lads, unchained or not
'twixt razor wire snickets or felled by Sassenach shot.

Bread Line

Bone-fisted, hard-pocketed
grub lines and tight, mean benches
gape deep-socketed.

Tin pot feed and foetid stench —
it'll do, *koledzy*
                    in a pinch.

Akhmatova

Where ignorant armies clash by night.
— Matthew Arnold

Murderous mad century, since your raging, raping army bled us
out on sanguine scapes, corpses stacked until seeming eclipses

who mustn't have wondered whether exists higher beauty
than this in faithful execution of art's lyrical duty.

Had I been near, famished as you, however fragile, howsoever frail
mightn't I have become an eye-gouged lover-painter in brail

frail hands tracing your agile, sacred mouth, your fine nose aquiline
not unlike chiseled marble martyrs risen from the Byzantine?

What faces did you spy in clouds supine under Moskva willows?
Whose esurient soul is so clement as to coddle who kills us?

Дорогой, you must speak further to us about the unforgiving way
of forgiveness when forgiveness remains evermore out of play.

Anna, O Anna, another age betrayed, we are murderers more treasonous
than yours. At Komarovsky, Anna, pray tell you yet well believe of us.

BUDAPEST

Profligate in a pornographic age, yet lovers do not
often lose each other, nor brothers, nor precious friends
sunk in yet another Stalin's taciturn permafrost. Few die shot;
rather, over-abundant texted oppression sends
all mortal meaning towards this overmuch of too much:
                                                            dot-
coms, crypto-currencies, engines of engines — dry ends
of Western Eurocentric xenophobic rot
where each floral, ruddy immigrant face offends.

Grim years post-Wall, in the cunning days by Budapest
greyed-out East no longer funding farce, each dog-weary face
jaw-gaped, enfeebled comrades sensing America's Godly quest
(preceding the patriarchal Christian's evangelical disgrace)
we tramp dirt floors trod flat between iron machines at rest
war-wracked men, women hard worn, and I...among my race.

VARSOVIE

Stop. Stand proper in autumn air before the '44 memorial.
Seek there to sense Ares's simple, implacable
greed. You will not succeed. Eyes that saw
death-skies seed fire sleep under streets once yellow straw
which rise in bronze, copper, glass glint. In that horrible year
when the children went, brash lad by fey, gay girl
puerile laughter morphed into relentless propeller whirl.

For whom turned from whom turned the gunsight knurl
was bloody earth turned, the dust falling, baskets filled with fear.
Fate. Destiny. You will feel no feeling at all, nor even awe
senses spent, rendered raw, unobtainable
human pity too dear, pathos a thing unsustainable.

Caught out, you'll pause, steer off ever so slightly disarranged
wincing from the rate at which your bank notes were exchanged.

Dominika's Song of the Ghetto

Mądry Polak po szkodzie.
> — Polish proverb

Flamed brightly pale, none so light as hearts dimmed darkest
betwixt iron-creased stones, fluttering like feathers.
Rended, faith's anarchists, dutifully did we love them hardest.

Guards elected small by large in no order — priest, peasant, artist.
Widows unadorned mounted mounds of rubble, long there dithered
flaming pale and bright. These lightest hearts dimmed darkest,

their assaulted silhouettes at dusk the starkest
popping like birches snap in winter's ice-girded wither;
marked by whom abhorred us, we blessed and loved them hardest.

Agnieszka writ names on cigarette papers, the district chartist
whilst we breathed of ash thick as sulfurous volcanic weather
and snipers aimed with bright blue eyes when hearts dimmed darkest.

Amongst us brave young men reeled, though their minds were sharpest
fallen unto despair, embarking, letting go their tether
so despised was goodness. How they loved, and we loved them hardest.

New streets now sleep in heedless ease; yet we leave the dogs bark loud lest
cities wake trembling should tanks again tread our wagons to splinters.
Burnt, we flame pale and bright, yet our slight hearts rise not the darkest.
Unwept, those farthest towards war, dark storms roar it: *Love them hardest.*

Thich Quang Duc

Unlearned, we leaned
                      unfazed
towards whom Huntley-Brinkley
                               named
black & white flesh inflamed, robes un-spun.

Famished, fire-tongues burned, spoke
vaporous, rebirthed
                    Buddha awoke.
Burn, *burn!*
             night's unblinking sun —

By Cathédrale Saint-André

Aliénor's gilded eyes spy
God's Aquitaine crusaders
raze all beneath blue-draped skies.

Dazed lovers cry,

For whom? Why?

Vampire

for Putin

...while we, beclouded by denial,
protect ourselves
from the blinding sun...
— Nina Cassian

Bestial half-human thing, you feed and fornicate, sight
children, rape women, obliterate, bury better men's wives
slaughter fleeing species, gorge on snuff-porn, delight
slink through dusk, slake of grapes, glut of honied hives
declare yourself Lord wherever gilded Aurora alights
weep not for whom vainglorious war all gain deprives
hoard each prize from which you take goatish, carnal bite
gloat of whores, homicidal life while no living thing thrives.

Say who remains to cheer empty echoes of a blackguard's boast
such as yours barked from ruined Ukrainian apartment tops
over dead troops, slaves, and girls? All are rendered ghosts
where penultimate, gravely-winging nightingale dropped
her quavering throat forsaken.
                     None mourn, each to toast
that your daemonic, malformed human heart seized, stopped.

An Ontology

Living things gollop
                    living things
sentient flesh or scalloped flower
entire and by the dollop;
thus men lollop, wresting
                        wringing
power from power
and so evolve until that fatal
fetish hour
            stings
with underworldly wallop
when those men, too
titan and trollop
are finally resolved, consumed
enveloped by lesser, petty
                    living things.

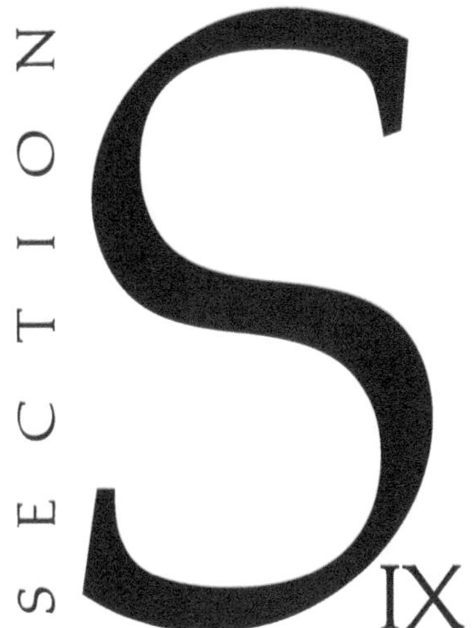

SECTION SIX

Samurai City

Would we were well away, long from Imperial City
Shōfu in sway. I weary of bustle and putrid decay.
This gay, green terrasse above thick, black
oxen in filthy streets
                    dumpling hawkers out the ass
carts and porters, up-and-comers seeking the Way
are but rings in Hell to me.
                        Here we go, Hakagure.

How little difference — scamper, delay —
that I go to snow his Council, shag the consorts
in his palanquin while colleagues genuflect
hunt for seats, samurais of bullshit walking
in a mercenary city. I was a right bounder
by lucre's opiate lured;
                      otherwise, no stay.

Flexed my wings, I did; learned to fly
close to the sun. It's all about the speed of
ascent, survival, odds of a bettor's rise and decline
whether you come out clean after saké wine
with maids-in-waiting, becoming a geishas' guy.

Stays fine in his cups during harvest call...

Easy, the sham guffaw; yet, politic
survival as all and all's survival.
                    Shall I pass
for a younger man, green
and fresh as new mulberry leaves?

Ministers stalk a gnarled and ancient park
parsing plots, bonus crops, golden trophies.
What then?
        Where shall I land, higher stakes in play?

In polished brass mirrors, I am my very logo
a brush stroke, breath of plum *parfum.* Cackling

across the grand pagoda
                              I savour
theoretical ego-death, unable quite to go there.

*They say they need new flavours, new divas
but I am not done if no new Kōbō Daishi.*

We live pieces of the whole life promised us.
The world is full of madmen. Power corrupts.
Already, future grieves our transgressions.

Such a fuss...

Shall I ply, with others towards war's increase?

Why do I bother?

How long hide a weak heart
                              this thinning hair?

Theatre is thus...

How to turn away despair, Chikamatsu, old puppeteer?

They speak as if I am neither here nor there;
such things are no longer my affair.

I do not think Nihontō weeps, cleaving esophagus.

Redoubt of Ravens

Pitched atop sacred temple
Birdbrain by Simple

sable ravens sit Zen
twittering teachings of Shin.

Proudly puffed, perching bird chirps
Why hunt what comes? Stay alert!

Soon reckons surly second
Tread not where Truth's not beckoned.

Squarely absurd, squawks the third
No ear's heard the sacred Word.

Fowlest four strictly insists
Thieves wrest but what's manifest.

Light on plinth, caws slightest crow
Find all you'll know by letting go.

Sentient six then joins the mix
Doubt's surcease is Faith's big schtick.

Seven's tweet resounds most sweet
Bright or bleak, true love's no cheat.

Ruffled eight half hesitates
Clever to hurry! Better wait!

Stumped, plump, preening nine opines
Ego-blind, who spies the sign?

Saintly last blasts to advise
Wise, lotus-winged farthest flies.
Boasts, lies, false Buddha drops, dies.

Wabi-Sabi

i. Wang

Halfwits three, yellow twits sit
hayseeds by low Yangtze loll

withered as morels.
Boys bellow, girls bleat, *You so lazy* —

Why such rush? Youth's wild zoom-zoom!
So we drink hazy

plum wine and drunken Tu nods
we were gods, rascals.

Her rare, pale flesh — an orchid.
Two mouths met, frail petals blushed.

ii. Li

Blundering dunces carved
tears with blunt tools, gruff-spoken
puffed we'd trod high, good paths.

Bad luck, we'd grumble
but lovers sing while thieves swing.

Winter gods scuttle
snow drifts through bamboo curtains.
Soon, cruel January.

Against the river, stacked cords
dwindle. Spring's rice wine stores
won't wet a widow's thimble.

iii. Tu

Seventy drained, buffoons chase
red crescents, race towards wane.
None gain their endgame.

Thin friends, our shoddy gimble
shot, we're no better planed
for one last true tack.

May, piled prune all
blackwood, waste hard hewn
hear — the spectral call of a loon.

We'll see no new tiger lilies bloom.

Lacquered Bowl

Night and I remain
late and tight
         spiteful wind chides
writes her name with rain
               — Shiki

Amber little Mandarin, say
why hang so long in wobbly balance?
Mayhap swayed shall I bend to you
and these fiendish, hammered cuffs un-pry
from wronged wrists, paper-skinned
warped and yellow.
               Askant-turning
quizzical, small and wiry, the crooked fellow
grins long at Yue Fei, puzzled
then rises in reply.

        Ai! Ai!
close along a shallow edge of the Eichi
under Zuiseki in Gen Prefecture
oft' I passed, injudicious, foolhardy
danced and cussed by tall fires spitting
sparks beneath sickle moons in airless July
and drank aplenty, loud-hooting, crooning
of feckless romance with lazy-
laboured women 'til quick day's
hazy settling hour lifted, whence I slipped
away to salute crisp morning's fine first ray.

'Twas a loon at play, but naught
came of it, seduced, resisting myself.
               O I do swear
assiduously did I vie, shying
off from great Shizu's fairest whores
lacking charm in a bumpkin's luckless way.

Straying, ai, of this was I sore guilty.
                              Thirsting
greedily I drank of a girl's disarming lusts
and lies when of a sudden the guard's alarm cries
rung neaby her posh pagoda's decorous terrace.

Gone, all gone
                gone with the running
green river's rushing song.

Thus I linger here almost in sight
in a dim, damp oubliette
true to the thrill of her, unwilling to forget
dark and piercing, blue-brushed eyes
or the comely, costly curve of figure
whilst betwixt black iron bars, surprise
new bluebells
                and bluebirds there
high in clean, thin
                unbounded sky.

Sun and Moon Born Lotus Sutra

White sun blazing thus
lifting dust where bottomless
vast sea tides once rushed
>— Han Shan

Those who claim they know, but cannot say, do not know.
Those who claim to say, but cannot do, do not know.
Only those who say by doing know the Way.
>— Lahktong Kyareng

WHITE LOTUS

Puck
        patrician
who most manipulates the new
moral model
                which picks and plucks
pockets in a manner not less venal
than a warground mortician?

Pilgrim
            prisoner
who circles most quick
that slow, labyrinthine path
which sends
                faithful and faithless
unto ultimate censor?

Prostitute
                politician
who sells, degrades
                        what is not
owned; whose pretty bed
and golden throne promises
false surety of redemption?

Publican
            priest
who draws the sacred draft
sustenance for parched souls
which costs
                the condemned
drunkard and deist alike
                        not the least?

Prodigy
            pensioner
who pulls a sweeter knowing
bow across the red violin

which plays dead
                    saint and sinner
through a gateless gate
out and in?

In the palm of an open fist
sun disk on moon disk
                    white lotus blooms.

Night and noon ablaze
alight in high forehead
                    the adamantine gaze
still-pointed, of an all-seeing eye
witnesses each display
                    profligate
in desire, impoverished by dread
annihilated in ten thousand
thousand ways.

Legions battle, unrepentinent
lords longswords rattle
hordes swarm, resist.
                    No man
persists.

BLUE LOTUS

ༀ་མ་ཎི་པདྨེ་ཧཱུྃ་ཧྲཱིཿ

Dharmakāya unfolds as Emptiness

Emptiness as Fullness Fullness as Famine

Famine as Yearning Yearning as Prayer

Prayer as Practice Practice as Stillness

Stillness as Silence Silence as Seeing

Seeing as Radiance Radiance as Mind

Mind as Non-self Non-self as Fear

Fear as Courage Courage as Faith

Faith as Grace Grace as Humility

Humility as View View as Joy

Joy as Fading Fading as Fruition

Fruition as Awakening Awakening as Sambhogakāya

Sambhogakāya as Nirmaṇakāya

Nirmaṇakāya as Dharmakāya

ཧྲཱིཿ

G
a
t
e

G
a
t
e

P
a
r
a
g
a
t
e

Red Lotus

Ploughman, baker, merchant
                              tailor
fletcher
          bodhisattvas
buddhas yet of apparent worlds
see, see
          always see —

Evaṃ mayā śrutaṃ...

Sentient beings are but supervening mirrors, feints
of form. Man's is merely a metaphysics of mimesis
projection of ground being. There is no sovereignty
of seeing or of seen. Red lotus on mirror pond
inherent existence as duality is impossibility.
Mirror is empty, not constituting nor comprising
nor containing what is reflected; one touches nothing.
Lacking dimension, image is arcing luminosity only
transient shadow. Mind is all; mind is emptiness
its own projection, vacant construct, *arc-en-ciel.*
To know the pumping of one's own pulse, too
is only mind. Mind is all and manifests as emptiness.

Self is also illusion, sea holding moon on wave.
Do not be conned by the grift of *over there;* all is one.
Nothing exists inherently apart from mind. Not *atta*
not *anatta,* not discriminated *skhandas.* Reflect
upon mirror, think upon Lotus Mind; understand
that and this as one taste born of emptiness.
Yet, were all empty, there could be no emptiness
And were all form, there could be no form.

Phenomenology of perception, vantage-continuum
mind is illuminated nexus of being and non-being.
Accordingly, all dependent entities are unreal, *shunyata*
delusive co-extensions of what is and what is not.
Of mind-as-vantage and apparent object, either
posited as autonomously existent forever remains
insubstantial, impermanent, ultimately unreal.

Dependent mind and object are vacant semblances
Ethereal appearances, ever only synthetic aggregates

not things-in-themselves, world as word renders
into what is no-thing, an incorporeal construct
reality as double negative, zero-sum. Mind's build-out
including mind as object of mind, are evanescences.
To see an object is, clearly, not to become an object
is not to become a thing-in-itself, no *Ding an Sich*.
Mind and self are conceits, reflected objects, as mirror
possesses nothing of its own. This is the nature of being.

Beyond form and emptiness, movement and stasis
Sumeru becomes shimmering cloud. All consciousness is so.
Lacking past or future, present has no ultimate referent
sits on shifting strata of transient sands already lost.
The far shore lies beyond enlightenment, transubstantiation
transmogrification; beyond prajnaparamita; realizations
outside space-time where one is both witness and Buddha
manifest. At the farthest reach, turning, one finds
only mind again, further emptiness, impermanence, paradox
neither bodhi, nor bodhisattva, nor Buddha; thus, Buddha.

There is neither before nor after, neither here nor there.
At the terminus of all dualities, without transition
without transcendence, one attains lucidity, the still point
of all knowing, all unknowing. Human existence is neither
fixed nor in flux; death is neither permanent
nor impermanent; one leaves behind all insubstantial
apparitions, attachments and anguish, an endless, naïve
grasping at a substantial world on this side of beyond.
Transiting across mind's dust-obscured surface, neither
nitartha nor *neyartha*. These very words are no-mind.
Such approximations are no more than reverberations
Resonances, echoes of echoes, stories of stories without
source, coda sounding to no score; not time, not space
but luminescent simulacra, inconstant sentience
quavering, illusory surface of imputed mercury moon.

All things are merest reflections, moon with no depth
on Mirror Pond. What was, what is, what will be
what is imagined or projected, all movement, occurrences
and recurrences, but a blink of an adamantine diamond eye
lotus petal shattering immaculate mirror. All is illusion.

No dharma, no dhyana, no dharmata, no dharmadatu;
no prajnaparamita, no Dharmakaya, there resounds

     Shanti Shanti Shanti

     शांति, ཞི་བདེ, 和平

primordial peace

               awakened peace

     transcendent

     will

     transmundane

     word

     divine volitional universe

     infinitely latent consciousness

     pristine emptiness-peace

     Rigpa

     whence

     to

     create

          create

     create

Intemerate Pink Lotus

Mirror Pond

Wayfarer
            wary one, willful one
Pluck up and put in your pocket these
Petals of the intemerate pink lotus.

What you envy must ever elude you
What you covet must ever possess you
What you vaunt must ever diminish you

What you mock must ever degrade you
What you shame must ever disgrace you
What you abuse must ever defame you

What you blame must ever accuse you
What you deny must ever name you
What you betray must ever declare you

What you abandon must ever attend you
What you hunt must ever devour you
What you destroy must ever vanquish you

Pink Lotus

Wanderer
            walking man, les errants, watch
The hoar-path, which so hinders you
The nether-path, which so hastens you

What you leave shall at last locate you
What you proffer shall at last enrich you
What you renounce shall at last render you

Monk or mercenary, migrant or Monarch
O Lotus, Pink Lotus in Mirror Pond

What we sheathe shall at last safeguard us
What we assume shall at last absolve us
What we love shall at last release us

Dreams of the Fisher

Murmurs of snow, frost snap
floats on canyon air.

Hale, once, we'd ply, pull bamboo rods
in the pale hour, far bell
                          sounding
flash of green Dolly tailing down.

Lithe-limbed willow
                    lets fly her dead
marks brooding, boreal wind's howl.

Less stout, we'll not again keep
to scouting out Spring melts swelling.

Deep cuts
          in autumn's felling.

Haiku, Tanka, Haibun

Grave monk pushes brush
stains chased by unthinking rain

girls rush, rouged in vain —

❁

Roar *Fin!*
      Cartwheeling
reeling, war-torn…
           Yameru!
yet
   plums, children too —

❁

Reel! Play!
      Lest you stray
lemon peel spun of sun spray

gay farfalla
     stay —

Boys paw no rope swings
today; crane-still

         strained in wait

all bawl out

      for Spring —

His tongue crosses breast
in cursive pens

        A lover's touch
is no palimpsest —

Little

    Devil's Cat

chrysalis, farfalla

      who

first twigged wings suit you —

Hoar-freeze cuts gale-gutted reeds
geese cleave high Vs
                        pale moon wanes
and no lover peacock struts.

Your true way linear, not
circling, askew, go…
                        Go soon —

Pond fills, daffodils
willows
            singsong whip-poor-wills

frond-clad girls preen, thrill —

Mauve wisteria
vines enthrall straw-haired girls, twine
loose truths, calm
                        June's hysteria —

Flaunt self-small honours
proud, loud man-fool, who fools call
fool.
        Fie!
            All goners.

Zoetrope, spun blur
tin machine plunged into whir
seen-unseen

            all mind.

In stillness
            Zen
            ur-

Plum blossoms disdain
all others; yet her pear tree
postures
            no less vain —

Carnie man scowling
knotted cord lashed to your staff
crack that quaking ape.

Ride your damned bike, he laughs,
RIDE!

Yowl! Yowl!
       howled Yi when it died —

❀

Hear
      his Guards approach
downriver, brass horns blaring
broaching Spring's mild peace.

There
      a second; three more…
Dear me, they roar
        the wild geese —

❀

My gallant, I ken
where to watch for you.
There, there
just past War Hill's end.

A neighbor marked you marching
coaxing our snow-dappled mare —

Slip of a glimmer
light pool a-shimmer
drifting mind
                    sprite fool

keen-eyed at water's edge, spy
unblinking
                Strike!

Quick white bird, green fry —
what was it thinking?

❀

Spare no rare pink salts
by Bhutanese mined; spread ghee
saffron as one ought.

Crest to toes, pour fragrant oils.
Pare your spoils,
                    vagabond crows —

❀

Trued to the wise grown
who happy thrive on little
glee gained not by size

Comes easy, joy, to whom vies
not
          unknowing-buoyed who knows —

Musk deer spurn us
                    (dusk…).

Fall's moon-brushed treetops turning
starlings
           murmuring —

⚘

Jigged, puffed
                gorgeous nonce
who swigged, wooed, procreated

once June-proud
                now, not so loud —

⚘

Dear heart, heart's desire
our hearth's gone cold.
                        Here, two coals.

Restart that bold fire —

R̶azor-beaked, kissing
cranes inch close.
                    Pinching green stoats

each thrills other's throat —

By mere weight of air
she declares seasons going.

Slight, spare
            fly, Winter —

Redbird undeterred
along came green hummingbird
blue titmous, too, whirred

Rigid line 'twixt seasons blurred
frigid Winter
                how absurd —

Winter's white-veiled hush
sea fog brushed ashore, flurries
riot.
        Memory-
steamed chamber windows
knots of hair

                silent, love's lusts —

Drifts, snowed-up stands bowed
hands paper-skinned, thin old mitts

Winter's ten cords spent —

Dare no hope, gloats pyre
gnash teeth, grieve her, not aspire

ash in air goads
                Higher —

Bashful geisha sighs
into bold soldier's shoulder

flashes of fireflies —

✿

Not matter!?!
                Frost-tongued
snow persists, stung by March rain's
gossip-hot patter —

✿

Snow clouds turn to rain
rain chills to ice, ice to snow

nor proud men remain —

Fig leaves drop, forlorn
hawthorn branch stretched to prick us

old hags bitch non-stop —

Wee boy, bonny miss
whisperwhispershisper

         SHUSH!

One plush, plummy kiss —

Lithe-limbed, green-new girls
supple as willow branches

Whoosh!

        December's whirls —

Fleet, purposed arrows
flown, geese drop from low snow clouds.

Priest sweeps stone, weeps, bows —

❀

Mirror pond, white moon
same not same, bright mind, too

        absconds

with morning

      beyond —

❀

By sleet's freeze cowed, veiled
hibiscus bows to pale earth

prays for proud rebirth —

Lilac blooms, laces
for girls
          who spies powdered time's

fine, tear-lined traces —

❀

Spring's weakness, boor pride
winter's, censored hope
                    I grope

she elides,
          we cope —

❀

Pale bloke stroke blue, pink
gloomy, gay
          bloom on snow.
                    Who
think joke true haiku?

April's twee love seizes
June's heat pleases, Autumn's stills

December
              freezes —

Spring, we made our start
hunting light in each dark heart
through bright Summer, too

then far Autumn, but 'twas stark
Winter knew
                    seeing's the art —

I would go with swans
mount the air towards blue snow melt

O these feeble fans —

Redbirds stopped today
stopped, but opted not to stay

Too cold, I heard one say —

Sunset scurrying
towards Christmas, wee fretful ones

watch, wait, worrying —

A red-headed finch
feeds in bent sunflower beds

fretting Winter's pinch —

Happy Christmas rose
blooms at its hour.
                    Our dour dead

assume such a sour pose —

Their sound below sound
snowdrifts mound, host missed lovers

Love's ghosts never found —

New blooms bend bowers
slake pouring Springtime showers
rebirth old powers

Forgot in these greening hours
the fading of the flowers —

Spare sleet covers rock
Lock of pleated hair in box

sleet smothers bare rocks

Snow mounts to windows
no count, a late husband's stone

cold day for widows —

Let the men have it
what Spring can't bear carrying

grim Mars in transit —

Plump plums of Summer
plucked, lost to maple cutters

young bucket runners —

Breath-stained glass, that track
pressed through drifts towards flat moon's disk.

O June, fetch him back —

Winter snowed under
(Summer wasted in wonder)

horded days
plundered —

MONOGANASHII

Each man's fleeting reign's
eternal, lavish, whilst
fixed in flux, the luckless

infernal dead strain.
Regarding this precedent
little petitions

to be said, parrot
though one does quasi-divine
suspicions. Betwixt

vain-lived, the all proud
in simple oblivions
of fulsome increase

and poor corpses wrung
out to dung in dull diminution
buddhas, gods, devils

each season's temple
rings, pleads: Brideshead to death bed
seek coalition.

SECTION SEVEN

Proust Beside the Seine

Pleats of goldleaf waters skirt a crooked place
gilt-edged birches outreach in balletic grace
bend to slake, but do not sound profoundest remembrances
for never were they thus.
                          Memory importunately abrades
away, mind's dots loop in knots of decaying synapses.

An over-long rumination pleading, *Stay...*
There was never another way than a fictive way
innumerable inconsequential occurrences of a day
become myth's continuum where there is no continuum
but a dream-dance leapt to the one beat of the one drum
now.
      Beckett was mistaken in this regard; no joke
waits for any man in a forever when of hopeless hope;
nothing drops in the three times. It's clapping
strings of Chinese fireworks billowing their acrid din
amid blue and red bursts of wrapping and smoke,
little more.

Hardly clever, I, nor cynic-quick, am quite the bore
yet stand prepared to prosecute who cranes to claim
he goes as Buddha.
                    Parents, and cousins of the clan
friends and progeny of friends, fast friends framed as
selfsame, our plain endeavor's misnamed as mystical
metaphysical.
              A father's father dreamt seventy strong
so too fathers, we scheme our seventy years hence
and daughters and sons shall spend their seventy-long;
thence, we cease to believe, life bears no further reverence,
lived in fervent desperation or in timid diffidence.

Traipsing just in stride

                    against this twist of Seine
a pretty thing it is, your virtuoso stroke, madeleines
yet up from velveteen sheets or the swine's appalloing stall
quakingh grunt, thrust and cut, love's grievous gutting's all.

Imitation of Life

for Nora

Elle avait les larmes aux yeux et était infiniment
heureuse de l'entendre respire près d'elle.

— Milan Kundera

i

Thinly blue striated clouds
slip through her
translucent afternoons

March-thorned hollies
brittle, new, prick against
bubbled leaden windowpanes.

Inanities and vanities
she was once as regular as
a biological clock. All now for whom?

Their quarterly *Georgia Review*
fumbles, falls idly
from frail, forgetful hands

to the wide-boarded floor
pages of a Mandarin fan
unfolding. Half effaced, she

misplaces, then recalls
the insuperable
dichotomy of bright and dark shades

which splits this first spring
from what was
to have been their mid-century fling

before besotted, illicit lovers
crushed her in chaotic
divorce. Of course, they were positively

lunatic. Fundamentalist and Jain
couldn't have been as mad
so oxymoronic, each glad

for the purest hell the other
would ineluctably pay
no Duty Free. Such uxorious pain.

Rodney Jones in Appalachia
Caravaggio and Klee
in a posh Atlanta suburb

he and she, say
could not have been
less alike or more maimed than they.

ii

What remains of the day, she thinks
to miss? How the wind hissed
on long spits of Ocracoke's narrow brink

roaring as he roared?
Packing out, there was precious
little remanded for her to adore.

Yet, when she holds trembling
slight new men
why regret him all the more?

iii

Clouds, translucent and thinly blue
thread lazily through
late, undramatic June afternoons.

An approaching storm's attenuated beach.
Two unhappy damned once hungrily
reached to enlace behind Nags Head dunes.

iv

A translucent pink Lauren suit, peaked
breasts and black V shown through
salt-white wave froth, he suddenly reappears

swept towards her on chilly seas beating.
A radio plays.
                    Heaven, I'm in heaven...
vanish like a gambler's lucky streak...

It is what forsaken spouses fear
scribing hearts on steam-frosted glass
high above l'Ecluse, vacant Gît-le-Cœur below.

v

All Sunday she sought soft angles of gilt
Paris in luminous galleries — Luxembourg
Poussin at the Grand Palais, *le Marais* —

but found only fellow queue-harried ex wives
en pose, scurrying compères complotting
forgeries and restorations of vandaled lives.

At the Salisbury

for AES

Die Hoffnung stirbt zuletzt.
> — German proverb

Mustn't a heart its very crux declare, one's part be voiced but once?
she beseeched over Chopin martinis, employing defiant poise,
spectral father hovering, precluding choice. No dunce;
yet, time had diminished her. *Shall I not be given to rejoice?*
Leaving med school post-abortion, she assuredly redeployed.
My longing not also be allowed, permitted just this once?

Lovers wooed, penciled dates, but Papa drafted sailors. Proud putz
paraded dress blues starch-crisp before his damaged daughter.
The doomed two attended Segovia while Hank vetted plebes, grunts.
She wept not, a heroic cover, when led to sacred Catholic slaughter.

His burial on boy's birthday, another of many redoubtable stunts.
False Stoic, proprietorial cunt, he bade no half measures.

Not the once.

Monastic

Odd, ostensible sins matins would sing to close
settle snug, sly, into dim corners of a sensible room.
Deep by decades, in thin wash of claustral gloom
rogue to rather side, far, faint, so fateful faiths impose.

Parchment-skinned, shored by shuffle, flagging will well worn,
knelt of plea in vague unknowing, night-wraiths' clag of song
pound impious No to Yes from beams hewn all of wrong
briar-bearers borne but halfway home under nail and thorn

Calvary's choice undone. Played out atop a devil's rock
daemonic clocks fast locked, nowhere ever, whether
now or never — *never!* — yield to impossible never-ever
who serenely weathers the noise of twenty centuries' shock.

Arise instead, cart the cloister's hellish weight as urgent tell
swells evensong's call, and rush — *rush* — not to crease the page
at requiem where pang and prayer purge graft's woeful wage
but chant you loud, *I am!* by cluck of tongue at Compline's bell.

Berceuse

i

Vêpres. Plush estates, lush in summer's verdant dusk.
Le Périphérique wends in and out towards Rambouillet.

Juridical black money, laundered peasants, cattle,
hunting hounds, and jumping horses put to hay.

Dogs bay, riders unsaddle, steel-shod hooves rattle
spark and clatter across cobblestone tracks to *l'écurie.*

ii

Saint-Germain-en-Laye. Unbundled girl dismounts mare.
In Le Marais, a round man fits himself into rubber wear.

Rue by alley, they trundle, sworn to confidential truths
no closeted confessor to bear their susurrus ruse.

iii

Glimmering contrails thread the infinite wash
needle-thin stitchings of pastel blue embroidery.

(Gosh...)

Mundane days, yet another day suspends. At an appointed
place, the clandestine approach, go pretenders unto pretend.

Gloved hands, brazen, sensuous, nor half so timourous, paw
the city's underbelly in a hole and corner crawl.

Who slips the knot of the all-seeing eye of God —
Annuit Coeptis — unlocks their subterranean way

to bars and clubs in the 11th, in gay quartiers
where counterfeiting is a keening sport.

(Let us play....)

iv

Luminescent contrails evanesence; day's light upends.
Polyman and painted girl fly in the twilit time, descend

into new waking time, the goatish time of plasticine dare
gloaming's furtive, fading hour, faceless faces everywhere.

Affair of the Massif du Néouvielle

And we thought that hour, that light and our long mutual look
Might warm us each someday when we were cold.

— May Sarton

1 | Remote Past

Remote in silhouette from below, a figure mounts
of a man by his own derision hunted, sought
fraught with false forgetting as he upwards gropes
griege tectonic slopes rubble-tossed, boulder-strewn
glowering over blazing flats of yellow rape
towards sharp ridge rings where, grey-green
a moss-hacked cottage sags lichen-mottled, its lintel
under snowpack bowed, racked at the ragged end
of autumn's going, grinding towards winter
on the Massif de Néouvielle
                              where fleece clad
herders drag straggling cattle off the wolds
and scalloped lakes and all ardours wane cold.

Seeking finer oblivion breathing cloud-thin relief
he pares a stick, carve of crayon, a marking pen
pulls creases of sack from his red woolen coat
wax wrappings of chevre from pockets and scrawls
odd ciphers wanting fresh words for loss
                                  animal-voiced
hound-expressions from whom begs to renew
with lyric sound by ravening ways wounded, feral
with whom loneness fought.
                        Moth-drawn to shivered hut
he weaves fictive tales of faithless ways and turns
through gauzelike remembrance reckless running
to hyacinth days and heart's dove drenched dress to flesh
wore striated rains and went from him unsure.

2 | Middle Past

Atop that distressed Pyrenean park, fanning spark
and ember, what strays through mind folds
among scree and cinder, lust for a life unquenched
burnt in flame slipping up the thick-sooted chimney.
He works wrecks of washed-out wood, litter
of torn books until his ashen, sack clothed essence
lifts towards black emptiness in that late season
scattered, misshapen as if an exploded constellation
nameless, trans-arcing undying godless skies.

Spectral outsider, he spies his half-formed mind, mind
beyond mind grasp back towards the straight true path
lost, which he'd not known, nor twice would find
without the pointing out of the Quaker missionary.

How he welcomes nightfall after the red slag
tittles depart their deformed and rotted trees
at dusk knowing when he strikes spare kindling
the thing alone that might free him
of the thousand stupidities precluding
hubristic man's lucidity
                         the gift puzzling and rare
she brought once in selfless bringing
whose empowered wisdom in its peace
along his pilgrim way gave patient allaying.

3 | Recent Past

Sudden the strange idea breaking
with laboured pain
                    of Bonnivard chained
captive under Leman, imprisoned beneath
those immense walls of sunken Chillon cave
sky-lost in his inverted, dungeoned rebel heart.

That towards infinite arcs he upwards starts
wrists torn loose from the lair, the massif's stare

unblinking
            of an instant in truer thinking
barren vacancy grown solid, full and square.

Bone-rattled under collapsed fractures of slate
and board, the ruins speak and, clear
he flees repose among rock and splinter
for he sees and hears and wraith-like leaps
diving down deserted planes, flown a thing farther
than name, a hurt beyond blood, shame
an ache behind hollow-socketed eyes, jumble
of legs disjointed, arms flat-veined
torrent in place of speech shrieking, ease of hearth
and heat gone in abrupt unforgetting
                                    for returns
the brunette curls, modest breast, creases laughing
at the living mouth, which alter soft
all hard edges, and that porcelain-pale
form naïve and waiting drives him
many days as he traces lost, chastely hours.

4 | Past Present

Downwards, down he rides geological pleats
down over fragments of shell, nautilus
abalone, coral
                and under towering peaks
vulture, ibex, and wolf roam free and fair
beside him unwary though in no known place
near no native trace, and with him hear
a sound uplifted on canyon draft, rushing
echo in reverberation.

Closer willful duplicity than dare yet compelled
blind to the course but rebirthed full waking
strong, emboldened force reborn, racing
across those humongous hills, he hurls
himself flying towards transfiguration, despair
bewept repaired, once again reborn

mortal madness done, and seeks that one
to whom he must bare what once she spake
in that ancient, shamanic voice gentle, spare
its breathless chant remaking
                              hovering in air.

Mon amour…
               M'amour, m'amour…

But where? Where?
               Speak! Say where…

until waking, perforce, he damns perverse gods
for she is not there.

Meteoric

W ords particulate
                        supercharged
plummet through ecstatic air
barrel towards green-blue earth
off lightening tongues of avatars
by blast and shock, purging nebular
crush of galaxies collapsing and shove
through warps of gravity crashing
fission-heated by which we see
                              believing
not in lazy lotto-luck, but blazing
stellar motes in heavenly hazel eyes
                               singularities
from which feeble, unwise men and mightless men
devise mindless, material heresies hurtling
pointless towards multiverses whence all
yesterly forces fly colliding in unimaginable
grandiosity
                 pressed, compressed
chased between space-times spliced, returned
again, bursting again, again asunder and then
arising unto each tomorrow's arcing, aching
race unforeseen, unforeseeable.
                         Fearless
phoenix, mythic bifurcated blades of beak
plunged into flesh without a trace, we watch
a faraway comet flung, trailing white-hot
sparks of universal will tearing, scorching
whole systems, broaching kills of atomic
muck across infinite pitch parsing.
                          Torch-burnt
blistering astral ember, we stand agape
at your all-devouring flame and turn towards omens
bading our species to divert, to duck

for we are become mere straw-men quaking
with desire, dumbstruck.

You, lover?
          You there
born of fire-sky breach?
                    You
who teaches the very flame
sudden in reach
                and I
after all?

We, who never heard
the clarion of your cosmic call
disintegrate in free-fall, meteoric
centripetal.

HARD THE TRAMS

Hard bashed the trams blast by bam
speed-smashed past barren branch of wham
gnash-fanged, glass-slammed
in fierce, slag fag-end days lashed
with slash of sleets December-damned.

Christmastime, New Year's, Valentine's
Day sting timorous, yellow faces dragged
homeward bound, gagged on crooked
camber off the rails, steel-howl, hack
and hash, disjointed clash, even
the hard man
           dis-
              membered.

For sight of spring, glad we would
launch stashed sacks of crisp new cash
off weary Warsaw's high-walled edge
to any warm and brilliant star pledged.

Far too glam a thing in its arrogance is
long-off April, how far, the too-gay
                      dash
that fête of life fleeting
                the merely flash.

Thus fraught, damned few wouldn't bend
sainted shams, martyred men
taught men
        caught up, wrung out
strung up, the dung-heap men all wronged
by sullen winter's slushy, wishy wash.

PALEONTOLOGIST'S LAMENT

We brushed teeth, flakes of faeces
revealed the scaled-down skull; but none
could place such a queer little species.

Latinates came, steering towards the Paris zoo
yet no one dares name
                              such a shy, simian thing
as this, which shinned high, ancient trees, braided
fronds of broad green leaves, repined
lazily, sheltering in cool, breezy ease.

Sleep, we inclined, in your primeval marais
                                        die at ease
now in glut of peace with jejune secrets, savour release
sweet relic of incompleteness recovered in clay.
Who among us doesn't vie towards surcease
dear, dead girl in a clean, dry box by the quai?

Timorous tribal host, we are envious
of long lost days for they were fierce and full.
Tend us, your progeny pitious
in their pedestrian postmodern lull.

Lang Syne Near

Strident strode bonny wee lovers violet-wreathed in heather
enbrumed on th' broodin' banks skirtin' peat-cut wither
by old Lairg's cozy stalkin' lodge in ancient Altnaharra
where title, fly, and date yet scribe each ghillies' ledger
guardin' length and weight o' slashin' ingot treasure
hauled from th' Mudale, pride o' th' barman's daughter
who guts, cleans, carves each maudlin fisher's slaughter.

Flame-purged by th' placid, burnt pyre o' Cawdor
embers spent, heaped in patina'd Inverness pewter
blanche no bones unblemished 'neath Highlands winter
hail-stung, weatherin' gales beyond th' old crofters' measure.
Keepin' tha' ashen yearnin' below softer tannic water
urgin', urgin' further; urgent in fear, *Here! Run! Hither!*
frantic she'll nae ken th' cry tho' sleepin' lang syne near her.

Gianna

…and that happiness leads
only to sadness.
— Io solo l'amore

Wintering through Prati, Gianna
wraps the long, pale, preening quills
of Dante's Hermès foulard, feather-slight
tightly about her overexposed throat.

The humiliating freeze of his leaving
leaches grievously into the mid-length
coal-grey sleeves of her monogrammed
silk-wool jacquard Louis Vuitton coat.

Burial

So soon, friend? Strip out the closets dress by dress
scarves, stockings, carnal laces adoringly caressed?

Delete in mock loss the last-slipped tweet? Or a card
in violet ink? *Let's lunch in the park next time we meet?*

Join me after, we'll climb down Hampstead Heath.
Later, a Gin and It, or tea and shortbread.

Which vivid remembrances become darkest dread?
Mornings? Trysts of an afternoon? The night's brideshead?

What reposte, old player, now she's sparrow-dead
turning a narrow London street, flash to the head

crack of cerebral lightning while, eider-light, life fled
its weight an absence, arrow launched into emptiness?

Come curséd weekend, the Connaught on a Sunday
tripping through the tube some Monday, dare you claim it?

Say it, then, man. (Say it.)
Her name. *Say!*
        O stunned, stony, woe-begotten git.

WHEN THE DEVIL KNOWS YOU'RE DEAD

Haply buried in the end by the new lie
dodged, stalled; but none thus inured construe
into more whats than what they're not.
                                        Milk-
purred, sham-spoken mouth by mouthful
gall and gale, the thin-lipped jaw
split by half stops, doubletalk in silks
                                        tales
of nuns and harlots, whose rebuking talks
upbraid through.
                Inflection points all, beyond the pale
skewed.

Likes of a crooked ilk bent as a yew
named and anointed sure and true
when the devil knows you're dead.

In the Cause of Shadows

Mes amis, *tous les fidèles,* we are given today to consider
fortunes of the less fortunate, our shadows felled before us
inexorably beside us, behind us in eternal, bitter
obedience; how they abide in melancholy ever thus
apparitions of ineluctable acquiescence so
lacking in autonomy, no volition of their own.
Dragged hither and there, we must own that they grow
flimsy, coextensive with whom cannot be overthrown.

Believers of the *royaume,* let us no more grudge their secret
obsessing over snowcloud, rent by raincloud, torn
between light and relief from light, their moony regret
a half-life lived in shades of night as they ourselves adorn
ever wherever we are shone. Lest one forget whose debt
is owed. It is ours alone, future fêted phantoms born.

EGLISE SAINT-EUSTACHE

Falls placid evensong, imperative upon each pious lily;
grave and turgid, thunderous antiphon blasts
round nave, choir, and deific pulpit willy-nilly.
Awesome, those ivory-yellow keys, pipes, and lasts
empyrean bellows reverberate, expiate all pasts
sins stuck fast in infinite manner of trespass (delightfully).
Heavenly, beatific heads, *pudique*, priest, and pederast
meditate, blessèd whether in balcony or high belfry.
Sacred and galled, gold-plated crucifix casts
immortal hunger from each grumbling, gluttonous belly.
For that precious hour, faint parishioners plonk amassed
prayerful for lamb shank, *saignant*, with English mint jelly.

Eternal souls, if peckish flesh, no immoral Pharisiac waits
quick to pinch *pièces Républicaine* to skint collection plates.

Their Good Life

after Sengai

Spoke to God, and glad.

G'night, Dad.

Dozed.
Woke.

Stone dead.

Sixty-odd, we'd 'ad.

BLINK

An instant to wake
an instant a breath
an instant, which baits
of an instant's rest.

"'Tis but an instant 'til death…"

Each man is left an identical fate
an instant to reflect, as all men ought.
If he'll have his due, he'll not hesitate
most men by their very reluctance caught.

An instant awaits on which no man sates
a cry no mortal soul has sought:

"My god, I've left the living too late!"

Many's the queer fool who'll not be taught
tooled by a life wiser men daren't undertake.

Plenitude of Princes

Leave it, then, all's done and said. Turn, turn
from outworn animus, turn from dread back
towards new learning. Learn to unlearn
faithful striding into staccato subtract
retro-discretion none can discern
but by that serene lean into future-tack
answer heart's urgent chuff and churn.

Glut you up on the very thing you lack
whole in emptiness, replete with yearn
glutted by loss of presumed mortal due.
Gather to you great losses all would spurn
before gay winning's weight was all you knew.

None endure such lattitudes of self-concern
as Prince Hamlet, each choice his plenitude to rue.

EIGHT

DOUBLE SONNET: MAN WITH WOMAN

i

Superimposed break on break, zinc and lapis tides break
into indecipherable chorales loosed on sharp, harpy air

rapacious wail and response. The bronze girl with Titian hair
and coral lips sculpts sandcastles, unaware of England's disrepair

which impelled a young king's life. These same cheered
him unto night at Agincourt, the failure of French seers.

Down concrete stairs towards a blanketed beach
one greets no fair, fleet heroes at the condemned man's reach.

ii

Tight to waterline, bussed tourists bathe in tea-green seas
bob up the waves, squadrons of invading hoardes.

Excoriating, ancient tongues forsake young lords
and Lydian voices shriek through foam-froth, ignored.

Bald, bulbous men once watched the flying curls
floating off the frigid shore on polystyrene boards

flipped in great white bursts, crashing wind-blown whorls.
Sand and shell, she glitters there, luminous in her Titian hair.

iii

Each autumn, we come to take this oblique Norman sun.
(There, look...a heron stops atop a dune and clucks.)

It bakes our faces palest pink, but none mark an endearing pair
on the brink, while we endure and endure, endure our despair

slowly strolling up the beige strand, drolly noting how undone
we've come, toeing sand dollars to toll our fare through flux.

I could not bear his falseness, their whispers, or the glare
bright and hot as a stare, of the girl with Titian hair.

iv

In Deauville, a clinic keeps him comfortably in his bed, if
dispirited. *Alors*, in God's care, we savoured a good life shared.

On the beach, I daren't neglect my not negligible good luck.
Alone, tracing the girl, seaward flung, with radiant Titian hair.

Postcard of Rialto Bridge

Savage Aurora; and after, her call flung predicted squalls
up Grands Augustins at the Seine's damp and filthy walls.

Room to room, he crops each step around each door
craning towards a knock behind which freeze the flocked

children of their gardienne leaping on carpeted stairs and
in the lift. Out moves a small grey man beside the band

with his tall African nurse shuffling off to Notre Dame.
Later, scanning the bouquinistes, twisting the heavy lock

towards its skeleton stop, he marks other times she has flown
panicked, to "old friends" in Venice overlooking a tight canal.

You live too fast, too light, her cream note read. She left
him in bewildered stasis, bereft; he wasted a hundred days

There came only her sepia postcard. How now replace
that cluttered, discontented space? *She might have said*

a friend replayed at Lipp, and so she should have done.
He nods redundantly, tripping over what he said

where they should have been had she remained; instead
delaying the shock he'd take, she urged, *Wait, wait, then wait...*

She would be right, correct or no, while he, stung
shifts among their bric-a-brac, a revenant, a thing undone.

Following CNN Sunday, he switches to BBC One.
Buoyant voices forecast further storms, decreasing sun.

Woman, Long and Walking

Elegant women arrive and go. Three were
most loved, with whom he spoke languid French
under beech and cypress trees copper-leaved
in lyrical, olive-gathering October.

There were strong women stalking game
two from whom he nearly recovered, lingering
late alone under constellations he could not name
in blue Junes, scythes of sharp sickle moons.

Long, he thinks, as Augusts conflate.
He'll not appear again that promising, fêted son
to whom all expunged faces now seem his single fate
but why regret bright stars through the death plunge?

A dexterous, decorous woman long and walking
punts volleys of chocolate-dark chestnuts
across Luxembourg park, the brown velour collar
of her heathered Harris coat turned high up

defying the season's 6th arrondissement trend.
Stuck mid-spin, his haggard face of cinematic stubble
by hers, porcelain, in sequences of sepia tones bend
behind a too-hot lens like blistering acetate bubbles.

Lex Talionis

for Renée

Came little drama from his murder. By single degrees
shockingly. Crushed by an RATP bus backing to the street
from its too-snug fit beneath the bridge. No one agreed.

Tangles of traffic, one horrific shrieking fuss
and an afternoon's usual delays lasted all of an hour.
Not long; one adjusts.
                  Bagging the body
drew tourists. (Shoddy). A halting old woman laid
a small bouquet from a wicker basket.
                            His death was lurid.

You schooled us all, admired the Court of Assizes. Who knew
what clever conceit conspired behind those clear grey eyes?
Cooly, faithless in false promise; trapped, monsieur hadn't a clue.

Discerning madame, you devise a fine demise, sublimely
plotted. A quick, clean nudge; a cinch. *Madame.*
                            I do not chastise.
All seal fast the vault of whom we are at last happy to despise.

Light Through a Sundress, Cooling

for Isa

I have remembered how once in Tintagil
You heard the tread of time hour after hour.
— Sara Teasdale

Parasols pulled, a slow sea-chop and slow, contrite
sea fog floated tour boats plying down and up from Cannes.
You nap at the Majestic. We touch via mail scanned
regarding agendas for the kids. Baths, schoolwork at night.

Shopping by phone, kinder asleep, neither scrapes nor flu.
Rain and wind in Paris, standard-issue afternoon.
You seek the most from Moore's Law, competitive boon;
I envy the teen life of our nourrice (who hasn't a clue).

We hunted each other. Not most murderous crows
warned us off our chase across wheat and poppies by Arles
steamy yellow sunflower canopy blazing upwards
umbrellas covering us where we fell into most lustful throes.

Early dark, a boy with groceries. Boxes fill your kitchen floor.
Sunlight sieves through a blue dress; you, cooling at the door.

Corbusier Reclining Chaise in Black & White

or

Proserpine in the Underworld
variations on Doktor Suzann

*I'll never understand it, are you close
To me, or did you simply love me?*
  — Anna Akhmatova

*If you entreat me with your loveliest lie
I will protest you with my favorite vow.*
  — Edna St. Vincent Millay

i. Bang

Lozenge Composition with Yellow, Black, Blue, Red, and Grey

Hung wonky in the American Hospital, Paris, B. bis 3,
attending patients waiting in Psychotherapy's 2-D lobby,
Mondrian is metaphor elicits an ink-blot effect
committee-approved, forcing reluctant viewers to reject
a priori skewed, non-contextual perspectives
while Kandinsky proffers his critique of squared objectives.

Subliminal social narratives should be framed anywhere but here.

Along the Xanax ward its vaguely out of focus clients never fully appear.
Hopper, Wyeth, Hockney, but nothing with Lucien's perverse flare;
instead, two-dimensional self-informed polygons, tests shared
without consent, the wrong boxes checked, stooped clinic guests
break the ice of private winters in unsuspected pre-assessments.

HR confirms all halls are to remain cluttered with Miro, Marc, Klee
for their patients' first stonking mogul-free runs on psycho-skis.

ii. Inflation

Mid-shelf, *The Village Voice* and an extravagant
illustrated translation of the *Kama Sutra*
behind a Louis XIV bureau in your minimalist flat.
There, a copperplate gravure, Dürer
by the daybed, the spider's web in my half sleep.
Already, you knew me too well. Flawless, after all,
Melancholia, tortured metaphor for those sessions,
and I clearly envisaged where they would lead us.

When it did so, and so soon, button after button
down your tawny back slowly, oh-so-deftly
there was nowhere else to go. Too sudden,
quite, but there we were, you and I; that
self-not-I spun fully up to be devoured.
         I felt
positively deflowered again and again, again;
yet, however far we fell, I found not a word in that
bruised mouth past the tip of your clinical tongue.

From my hypno-trance I mused, *Such beauty*
was never young, and thought, *flawlessly German,*
and the smokey Gitanes voice as well.
        Thus we moved
towards further appointed rounds, but I had no choice.
You coaxed, plucked barbs out of a psyche deeply stung
deploying mystical, psychic-seer arts and pop song hooks
as easily as flipping pages in your annotated leather book.

iii. DARK AGES

Doktor Black

I must tell you.
                    I prefer you care less
about the cheque than my finer mess
this desire arising on a mid-century couch
in a classic Haussmann flat.
                    I float out
into unfathomable black eyes, impossible
almonds in an antiquely sculpted face leveling
its look of artificial grace when all is merely
academic.
                    An *amuse bouche* for you as old hat
as that. Is it an addiction to risk what blinds
my eyes wide shut? Were those not ropes
of dark hair about my wrists, or a pro's tropes
dangerously, then fatally, leading to a darker abyss
of heaving cleavage between heavy breasts?

Among many books, Ch'an from high Sung.
There is no ox, delicious Jewish princess.
What bi-polar shock set you flying off
into therapeutic nothingness, your *néant*
fleeing Berkeley for a posh Parisian flat?
Such immoral splendour in the sanitary 17th
clutching only an empty calendar.
Post-partum, dare I look while you undress
at the terminus of all our sessions?
O let us, then, list the lessons
of our synchronous
tumbling together.
                    But first things first, n'est-ce pas?
(This one's a cinch.) Never, *never* trust
the French. They sell their mothers to save themselves
having to cross la ruelle for a stale baguette.

Next, do not forget
despite deep longing in lonesome eyes some will
not be healed, hungering — *trust me* — to die
under the wheels of a box car filled with lies.
                                        Last
whatever you do, tend not towards infatuation
with your therapist. It is a refuge known to be
bloody, one of recrimination and regret.

I, Doktor? I grow unwise in hapless gladness
for these thrusting lows and highs, your
false falsettos, your historic histrionics. I
have heard them all, craved them all
in my cadaver suit, rigid as rigor mortis
coming clean like cremation
                                        Only
it isn't happening, can't happen like this
not here, nor now. Stagey joker
my sweet, sardonic God, the endless wobble
of my moral gyroscope, want's heavenly,
oscillating mechanism pounds inexorably
back towards childhood triva, towards juvenila.
We chew our schisms as cows masticate
fattening pretty, plump, slaughterhouse asses.

Ah, you girls who wear glasses...

Say, my muse, do we dare? Do we pass?
There is only one end in each aria's belly of breath
high pitched into your theatre's plush, private air
the arc-lit alleys where choruses of papier-mâché men
turn out of drab offices dragging the fox wife's hymen
through empty places where no audition wins.

So it begins again with *I confess*
the unequivocally predictable, a *Yes* for you
with Christmas trimmings hung on a dying tree

among unopened precious things.
Going
I meld with the chimney smoke, these flowers
swirling into ghosts of unknowing spectres
our start-and-stop calls, the terminal clack
following a too-considered line, saying
Want of meaning leaves love predatory
its cost not less than all, which yields compulsion
precisely because love is impossible, secondary.

Technically speaking, what else shall I repress
blue dove? To how many others have you
shilled the psychological thrill of that voice
a thing so pure it can only mean business?
I do not believe I am your only witness.

iv. EMERGENCE

Knots of Thick Black Hair

Your *ascenseur*, it rings like Kyoto bells.
There's overmuch seeking of the epiphanic
elation, a cloistered monastic Dharma
of therapeutic prayer resounding
through atmospheres of delicately lit air.

Positively heaven the way your long hands
draw back knots of thick black hair. Surely
you understand you're a hemorrhaging cost
following an ampersand.
To what end,
my symbolic castration? Your notes, my
churning; the razor cuts, my blank yearning?
Our lack of will goes down like glass-
edged pills, your astounding, *Go! Yes!*
against my beastly bellowing foundering.
No!

No! No more! (Not less...)

Princess, how keen, your precision, this
fractal despair, our oneness as I careen
towards your eggshell undress, your zealous care
under high zinc skylights breached
by spare, late February sun.

                              Doktor, you become
more insightful with each dare,
most penetrable just there, pretending
you are not utterly aware.

v. ORDER

By Whom I Was Returned to Future Black

Madame, you faithfully honour our hour's
appointment, but always when I no longer need
you. Tell me
                  my insupportable rock
where were you this morning at two o'clock?
Did you nose no angst up your circular stair
or do you relish the impossible unknowing?

God, I have done so much rowing...

Do you count the bleats of sheep in the 17th
or the money we pass, no amount of mercy's greed
enough? Do you revel in my mourning, that I
marvel at your lusty touches, awed by your
cynicism while I unravel?
                              You must be thoroughly
overcome with the pointlessness of your repairs,
the endlessly clever counsel I so seldom heed.
Tell me, tell me, tell me, *do,* Doktor
before the long French holidays, where
shall I hide when you fly off to summer affairs?

Pray, will you quietly say my name
with a humane, soft-focus stare
and dream, dream, dream of me

our exquisite excess, supine upon the sand
of a blistering Aegean beach
unwavering problematic far out of reach?

Blush and think of your illicit lover's duress
at one o'clock, three o'clock, or in drowsy waking.
I shall imagine the biting flies that fan tides
with their trillion wings and the easy sweat
on a bounteous chest, beyond mistaking

while it rises and subsides.

vi. EXPANSION DEATH

Fade to Black

I've lived long, Doktor, have known many women
but none by whom I was so relentlessly forgiven.

Yes, you've lived a life and have had others
claiming some. One wore metal studs, hell-for-leather
one, saddle oxfords and socks to please her mother.
A third opened to you in turquoise Corsican water
her skin oiled and bronze. You were fond of her even
loved her, but were as you remain, in horror
terrified by commitment, suspect of their mothers.

O Doktor, you are invariably there with a hunch
after we've enjoyed our lunch; never *impromptu*,
never when I seek you not. Tell me.
                                    Be clear.
Where were you, again, at four o'clock?
Do you suffer the decline of my psychic stock?

I am neither charlatan nor magician; do not redress.
Yes, your paramour but first your clinician.
Scanning your semiotics, I did not plan this spin
beyond our finite space of consultational, "Begin."
Yet, tout à fait, each word has been a lover's caress.

Reaching for a kiss at La Bonaparte over brunch
say — you *must*, Doktor — where shall I go
to heal myself of the cure
for all the ways I shall adore you when
you vanish into July's retreat? With whom
shall I whore in August

                    your gulet gliding offshore?

Not now nor in any time. We endure each other's
obsessions. Go, stay; as you wish. You have free will.
It's nothingness that haunts you, its vacant power
draws you even as I usher you out the door.
This was our bet, our sweaty gamble
to bleed you dry or leave you in shambles.

Months? Weeks? How long before
one of us breaks, surrounded
by floral French décor, astounded
under these ornate ceilings
on my zebra-skinned floor?

vii. FUSION

Consider us, Doktor, from Symi at Rodos
its steep, amphora-strewn, aquamarine coast
Panormitis at the harbour's entrance, or rounding
Bodrum towards Attica into Aegea's glory
promise eroded like columns on a promontory
where tourists breach bright, semiprecious waves.

Counting out crises like ancient Greek coins, I
stagger at the fragility, the insignificant size
of our imploding state, its infinite weight
in your rain-small hands pulling me to reprise
last week's exoneration when your pursed
your pouty mouth inviting me to take the plunge
between perfumed Greek thighs and all
the therapeutic truths we can never expunge.

Chair to chair the playing's the thing, to start
and stop, then start again in envy, in hunger.
I pick up your electric wire, its current
jolting between us. You deflect, then inspire
my flaunting every danger.

To what shall I aspire

when but ash remains of my Hindu pyre?

You lose yourself in illusory symmetry, in delusion
are the Minotaur in its maze, its labyrinth
the Wittgenstienean lie of reason.

Ashamed then proudly

melancholic in inverse mimicry, you cry
out for these hits of milky, motherly lingual art.
Gorge, feast on me, eat, she said, *savour me, try*
a prick of scientific sin as have I. Swallow the bite
of irresolvable famine in my analeptic zero-heart.

viii. SINGULARITY

Infinite Black

Thus do I ceaselesly return

home

as it were, negligibly off, always
hers on the mend. It is purely
psycho-craft, *kintsugi*
and I, glued together in shivers
by golden, dialectical *uruhsi.*

With distance, I see it
as an unteachable art known only
to shamanic masters.

Positively Pavlovian

isn't it, Doktor's willful
antithetical reconstruction?

Sheets, by prescription, wrapped round me
we, heretical scrivenings of pen on paper

a visceral rewrite of a psychological caper
enabled, precisely executed by all-too-willing
hands then again, again, again disabled.
                              It's ever
my head in the clinical oven
that cat-purr of words, my being
tragically dragged back in a scarlet mouth
where, clearly mad, never fulfilled
it all goes south, and I in the role of harlot
cracked catastrophically, jubilantly
                              apart.

Hommage à '8½'

We quit rue Christine uneasy, little said
Mastroianni, the very morning, dead.
Many came with grand bouquets
wrapped in green tissue and cellophane
placed at entrance and issue of his flat
in Place Saint-Sulpice.
                Dismayed, I paid
a joyless priest, fast with words, who christened
our wailing boy in unformed voice pulsing
through that vast and plain cathedral.

After, we took drinks, feeling rather dull
nodding child and recently deceased
at teeming Café de la Mairie.

Then were close when poor Charles came
to fetch the remains of heart-rent Diana.
The hearse paused, dark, vacant
                      returning
later with a simple wooden coffin
predestined King henceforth defeated.

When villainous Mitterrand went
the old boys, *Résistance*, wept
Vichy at last spent.
Evil is wicked-clever, François
even dead, a cunning devil.

Each year, I visit Bonaparte's
colossal marble sarcophagus.
Ambition exceeded him. All die
lesser men, leviathans, myths.
Toxic, even his tenderest touch.

Lipp, de Flore, Magots —
all evoke adored memories.

Tin *deux chevaux* overturned, upended
inviting streets burning, and Sartre
on his boulevard
                              delighted.
We dreamt of Gallic gods suspended.
He died leaving *trop peu pour le coeur.*

If blank night claims these
Claudinalle, Fellini
charming Mastroianni's art
(He greeted guests so breezily…)
then there is no saving us.

You mix sacred and profane
too easily
                    she complains.

My darling, so little here moves.

In our great, grand 6th, God's quartier
one learns soon enough, doomed
affairs make much public fuss.

In Paris, Death
                        drives a tour bus.

Zinc Bar

Clamourous, cool, the zinc bar's edge
cup and cutlery clattered, hammered
there and in dampness here clutters underground
wedged into shade beneath ochre lamps.

In-between men, hard men in flat caps
voices stammering on the binge
meaty digits gone copper-tinged
roll short, jagged, filterless fags.

Joyless the hag girl's rag boy
flaps fat, soft jowls unhinged post nap
ham hands round hard-nippled breast
snuffs his uncoddled proletarian howl.

Thick pick and trowel men and welders ravenous
turn in urgent, sweaty witness
                              biological, lecherous.

OF NUBIAN HILLS

The nakedness of woman is the work of God.
                              —William Blake

Merry foreigners in our morning,
we laugh, we touch each other...
                    — Gwendolyn Brooks

Ai!
half wry
lost to spry
nor wont of die
where damfool men vie
hound no leopards up high

prize
not lies
but surmise
the square man shies
off sophistries, cries
Swat! to salacious flies.

Fie!
say I
lust's own spy
who'd zealous ply
she-devil's goat eye
by gloat of goatish sly.

Seize
it, prise
Why? from vise
want's jinxed lynx rise
no slinking disguise
blinking jealous, unwise.

O go, accede, not apprise
outfolded Rift Valley thighs.

LIMERENCE

Secreted green garden
                    green moss-encased
tossed among granite-grey glories
covert in shade by Santiago de Compostela
lost unbidden amid coarse blocks and keen-storied
buttresses braced in announcing
                                your heady wares
weave these wonderous, twining
gay garlands of oza-blue wisteria, thread
finely spare new leaves through
                        Tereza's flaxen hair.

Unbounded green garden
                        whose colours
deliquesce round black irises
which iridescence in raven-
sable eyes, frame the wilted curl
the single doused, draping tress
draped down the lobelia-blue dress
of a woman no more a girl.

Sure in this one art, pure
Czech face ecstatic, so slight
so square, Tereza's raven-sable eyes
liquid
        see her bright glare
under thunderous shower delight the air
an hour's streaming traces inciting
further fulsome bowers
                        burgeoning.

Unwed from want's worry
how she savours there
each flower flourishing
                        in jealous chase.

Do not stare
                nor dare her fury
declare not, nor look upon a titan's
                                emphatic face
for whom diffident wind is merest
trifle of amatory worry.

O do not tempt that rare
                        withering glower
from jubilant sable gaze of flaring raven
with graceless, greedy dithering
in a lost green garden haven.

Disturb at gravest risk fair
                        serious Tereza
but witness there her
cognatic, coy
                Bohemian power.

242

MASKENFREIHEIT

(Deconstructed Sestina)

You're an expatriate... You get precious.
— Ernest Hemingway

Give him a mask and he'll tell you the truth.
— Oscar Wilde

After-flash Les Halles, the thunder murmurs
mythopoeic gin-rain cracking silence
nick-knocks, and desultory talk-talk
bar girls blubbering through murders of tears.
There's nothing here but lousy takes
among cluttered tables, shifts for rotten stakes
in coal-brown air where pock-scarred
nighthawks with shank-thick wrists place
hand to broom, cart bins then clean
up to go.
        Verily, they leave no trace
broad, beery men with Cytherian women
walking de Chirico streets, deep-cover fakes.

Only there's no more telling
chubby, cheated sheilas from fakes
stalking miscegenated markets, snapping
tendon from kill in a butcher's silence
sad bastards no polyphilopro-
genitive Catho dare backward trace
packing their tinsel, trumpets, wreaths
under dim, dense skies weeping angel tears
to canticles sung by mendicant
mercenaries in a half-empty place
weary chorales flung for the bucket-red
charity of grim Salvation Army stakes.

Saturnalian, we mount our great yule tree
until the children shout out for guys, stakes.
Bunting and balls strung kitsch-high
bloated Seine's boats fill with fakes

motor a dirty river's winter waves
pale-skinned punters haling each new *place*
their Norman Noël's electronic
German lieder breaking silence
and soul.
        At Saint-Julien-le-Pauvre
poor sainted Mary's woeful tears
fall through cold, tumescent air
antique pews void, no mortal trace.

Lost to her diminutive garden
faith thin as rubbings tourists trace
dodge holiday traffic stuck at the zero-hour
vampires dread the hardened stakes
along crowded quais, none recognizing
foreign voices (or their tears)
under green lead and copper spires.
Notre Dame a line of paint-stripped fakes
bleeding reliquaries, replica saints
lit by *cierges* flamed out in dingy silence.
We in bistro exile are merest
ghosts, I think, in a spectral place.

We preen, posh flats profitably flipped
like bobbing peniches with no moored place
and ragged men, *gitans*, rogue
men on beaten bateaux mouches trace
the foreign exchange with shameless Yanks
titanium hip sockets flexing in silence
with new fluidity in secret streets
untethered for a while from suburban stakes
along the sidewalks by the glittering
tall vitrines of Samarataine, its fake
cordoned boxes empty as clockwork elves
on crystalline drifts of Swarovski tears.

What alien voice is not unlike our own
in the end? We share their tears
hear them chatter —

                    It was too marvelous a thing
to discover that unsuspected place
in the 6th, n'est-ce pas!
                         Yet the luminous stalls
of Saint-Germain blind us still with fakes
beside its small, medieval église
where nameless chiselers once traced
tears onto stone in awe of an evangelical
wager's impossible Catholic stakes
while elegant polonia trees in chic Place
de Furstemberg sway and pray for grace in silence.

Morning light's doxology, its pneumatic bells
break the artificial silence, bring automatic tears.
Hydraulic hammers pound soteriological stakes
prop each arrondisement's most sacrosanct place.

Masks, Peripeteia
die Maskenfreiheit aus.
                    We trace
lost brethren by our rarest masks
urgent, unchurched fakes.

DER VERRATENE ENGLE

...et je ne pense pas qu'il y ait une seule personne que j'aimais
que je n'ai pas trahie à la fin.
— Albert Camus

Convoke no congregation nor requiem call.
Nor hint of their murmuring, those lavender roses gone.
Turn none out, all tapers dout; put back the phone.
Invite paid mourners as needs must; settle them well
but refuse all weeping otherwise over the littlest bone
tangent-angled, plumb to apostasy, which God so appalls.

That he is dead, pray, leave mum the Sunday bell.
No tower's bronze and tongue are paired to atone
with a stroke for this rare, iniquitous sin.

One twilit hour more, his worst shall be undone
when long denied due honour she will be hither flown
who, cruel betrayed by borrowed pledge, in sorrow fell
from such a far, dizzying edge, the buoyant air so thin
new faith, that naïve, devoted thing, could but her woe dispel
whose true heart languished, lost in faith to faithless men.

Through Vapour

Dante Alighieri put this man in hell
for that he was a stirrer-up of strife.
— Ezra Pound

Rended stars portend spent, sallow things ravening for resolve
men bent on diminishing gain, no flying Baryshnikovs but gritty
undead weight unformed, unsought, with wanton futility fraught.

Girls of summer draped in unnerving beauty, quick, pretty
leap as dancers ought, launch lovers through voids of vapour, relay
Rended stars portend vacant men at the verge, purged of all resolve.

Dolphin cries before cleaving prow caught in breathless net, empty
in the thin, salt air that dries its liquid skin. Dying, it is not
undead weight unformed, unsought. With what futility has it fought?

Tiger raging, tamed to breaking, clawing chains without pity
paws at its keeper's leash, gnaws its maimed pegged limbs, growls
Rended stars lament spent tallowy things, maws of toothless resolve.

Loop-legged homunculi, clowns and freaks in a circus city
of streets, parks, unrelenting still they dream to swallow fire, saber
undead weight unformed, unsought, fools by fate's futility wrought.

Vanquished Gerontos vying, will wasted on plains of war's atrocities
decry shackling truss but dare not brave whether they were thus.
Rended stars portend straw men, hollow men spent suborning resolve.
Undead weight unformed, unsought, lorn they fade, horror-fraught.

OUR TOWN

for The Great Paul "Butch" Andrews

The Old Man leaves his Road to those
Who love it no less since it lost purpose...
                      — W.H. Auden

Madness...

           so soon gone.
Left, we chant your antiphon
pleading,

           Why go on?

Tamp sad cierges, tug the shades down,
ignore the phones.

                 It is no more, our town.

Croissants et Confiture

Cosmos conspiratorial, all space-
time a cautionary, incomprehensible
infinity scattering treasures
of lives, lovers, losses
collects at the bottom of a small
Café de Flore coffee cup
in measured white emptiness
while hyperkinetic passersby
wear near-infinite fullnesses of
extravagant leisure, well their due
have not a clue either
with regard to collapsing
and expanding others
concurrences
spinning out amid
cacophonous
porcelain clutter and
metallic clatter and
unintelligible
chatter and stutter.

Woman to woman
as it were
les vieilles femmes fatale
set small and round
among round and small
green and white tables
aligned in long, chaotic order
upon the achingly bright
trottoir piétonnier
come sunny, summery May
replete, one might say
in practiced pose
under rare, rich bâtiments squarely
placé along the brilliant, blaring
boulevard in golden
rays of careless bullion light

sacrosanct to these their Sundays
sedate and secure, refracted in pure light
contiguous arrondissement cliques
inured to the imperious hauteur
linger unhurried, *chic et*

                              étourdi, très

chic, très, très chic

                   un système
parfaitement achevé, parfaitement
bien, partfaitement inégalé
à pluperfect Saint-Germain-des-Prés.

Soldiers of Fortune

I love the bitter and the rude, the drunken,
The tramps and thieves that skulk among the shadows.
— Iris Tree

Île de la Cité deploys riot-ranks of peripatetic hosts
scratching, wobbling on crutches, clacking braces
teetering off to beggar races.
                              At peeling lamp posts
in historic doorways, men with corkscrew faces

deaf-mute boys by angular, palsied girls, blind
Africans, the one-armed Kurd, savant
with a touch of Duruflé (less his mind).
Soldiers of fortune, storm troopers on the rant

sweep ravenous across Champ-de-Mars targeting
maneuvering, flanking, outflanking
tank caravans of Russians in German cars, sweaty
vagrants moving on Ritz and Crillon bars, ranking

chalking tactical references with insurgent eyes
scavenger scouts at the edge of Place Vendome.
Do your boots not feel tremors in heave and rise?
Fiery hubris feeds, iron hooves pummel the Tuilieres.

Four tramp hard in gallop and charge
                              hurtling home.

Souvenirs

Late, by decades late, generations late, come.
Come in any case where none present in your brochures.
Under Montmartre's topaz sky, buy your fake Renoir
pretend you were there, in Saint-Michel or leather Ritz bar.

When the green metal stalls of bouquinistes lock shut
against night's vagabonds and thieves, come knowing
you might have been the boy in half repose on granite steps
clasped to a lithe-waisted doll long with bare, brown legs

loving cool, fast, full by dismal December's snotty Seine
embracing, devouring his girl. Come, not to slip off
seeking postcards or football contests from Spain via satellite;
rather, deep, dive deep, then deeper into narrow, fetid streets

papers and chairs from emptied attics heaped
beneath postered lamps throwing stained light onto yellow
sheets of an expatriate's *Herald Tribune* blown
smutty into a turgid river against its water's dreadful walls.

Nothing left for it, no new mistress to retrieve
arthritic-grown, bent in disrepair, couched in irreparable grief
agèd, overthrown, then plunge into the never-what-it-seems.
By Mont du Souvenir...dead saints, dead soldiers, dead dreams.

Rapture

Up

Let go, friend. There is someone near to arrange it.
That, this, the thing you simply *must* get done? No one cares.
Décontracter. They'll text you about the Schlumberger shares.
Annuities spreadsheet? Trust me; doesn't matter a whit.

Like you, I worried, too, apprehensive when suddenly haled
feeling watched from every corner by some winged Kim Philby
uniquely theirs in a badly cut Russian suit and tatty trilby.
I writhed, angelic moth, on a board by moral pins impaled.

Early, I remained convinced I'd inexplicably been burned
spurned, the purgatorial gates had been bolted behind me.
It's part of the vetting, yes? Of course, it gets to you, agreed
but they're concerned we remain fully unconcerned.

By chance, late yesterday along the beach, I ran into Updike.
He understood. He's one of few with a feathered back. (Schooled
though hardly as sainted as he seems.) Such are our scheduled
serendipities. Presently, we await arrivals from an H1N1 spike.

Nonetheless, patience proved, up/down cleft wholly riven
do you not suspect, vaguely sense, we are, *ahem*, superfluous?
Their very banality! Everywhere the same slack, supercilious
smile. Tell me, pal, didn't you clock it? Quite the lockup, heaven.

Down

No matter what blessings befall in this place, you
will negotiate a better price. You'll find someone who'll buy
anything for more. Following the gaunt, grim march to die
after their grey guards take the long gold teeth of the Jew
ell what's left. Sell to the French. They'll buy, deny all.
Goes without saying, Americans finance, take major cards

as do the Brits. Move only by inches, by half yards.
Plead a newbie's naïveté, show gratitude. Above all, stall.

Hope, faith, the kids — what did you expect? Not here
but...*where else is there?* At all costs, move along
knowing when you arrive that everything must be gone.
The end is no end. One feels more than a little queer

but keep going a step at a time. They're always ahead
of the game. In perpetuity, cities, countries tumble down.
Grin through collapse, shame; none like a frown.
You must trust me. You'll soon thank God you're dead.

Indeed, get ahead, but not in haste. They eat dignity
here in any case. Lose yourself in a clean-scrubbed crowd.
never speak your name or say any true new thing aloud.
Believe! then assume the Devil's humble iniquity.

Between

Waaal, yes and no. The trouble with Wittgenstein
is his presumptive logic, the interminable volubility
his syllogistic twist. But so much for Philosophy.
Synthetic neurochemistry's now the end of the line.

Fruitless centuries struggling towards nexus-plexus
the smart of the matter, our spouses growing daily fatter
down the hole we flew, politely sipping our bladders
full of Mad Hatter's tea. Even the poor BBC's in flux.

We're getting nowhere fast. I should say, *faster*
at the numbing, reason-defying speed of Twitter.
(Which, I've twigged, is fast.) Accumulating digital litter
electric mourning becomes us, Gilliam a master.

Ludwig, poor Ludwig, that long, linear thread frays
a metaphysical disaster. His lingual, not-quite-tight noose
hung us out like a girl's raggedy doll loosed
on anemic academic winds tolling ballparked end days.

O we mucked it up indeed, friend, despite the green
offensives.
　　　　　But what the hell? Dumb luck plus
chaos may yet yield order. Whatev…we missed the bus
neither up nor down, lolling in sour limbo, ever thus.

Between.

La Jeune Veuve

Moddish while meek, who once heedless wed
at this votive hour now woe-besotted, sour
marks dear departed's susurrate bed
with gay flowers.
                Long-staying, lamented dead
under wild musks mild with rot, urgent
wire-locked jaws pray unto their author.

Boys a-scurry
              girls in girlish worry stare
then flare from the familial plot and turn back
smiling at their name recessed in stone.

Towards breath of musty vestry air
pungent incense burning, no holy plea
quells the young widow's yearning.

Beneath his placid bowers her
untamed voice, lionhearted, swells
among the bronze, towered bells.
              Vite! Hurry
mes enfants! Vêpres! Vêpres!
           Vêpres…

PERSEPHONE

Upward braid faithful tendrils twining your low grate
in extravagant, erubescent display while I berate

and pluck all bright claret flowers towards sun turned
to Sunday's round imaging they might have learned

better by fading September, no hummingbird soon
to savour them, nor honeybees alighting by the noon.

This first crisp winter siege wild off frigid bluff
seizes shaken trees where flakes of sepia leaves scuff

and crackle under foot while sudden and sharp its chill
schemes to sneak beneath each shearling vest. Willing

our wayward circuit home to fill your vase, neglected of late
my meager heft of blooms and I decry fiendish, slutty Fates.

Who fiddles loom, places pall, fixes a final plait
matters not. Pale bloodless moon and I bereave, distrait.

We wait, bereft
              and wait, wait...

SPIRALING

for CH

What will survive us are shoreless seeds and stardust.
— Maria Popova

i

Stripped beds, curtains rent, twin placards bare
furnishings lent before our denouement
there.
 Badly bought, bitterly effaced
it is not the debasing pain endures
for not the darkest heart such a thing
as ours outside time abjures.

Where is the word one wants to start
the retelling when come no words to say
of that spare space and lovers gone their way?

None care, forlorn in ceaseless attending
in forsaken, unforseen pretending
every resource spending even
now, years after loss of grace.

Everywhere, I see your face
and there better knowing extends, exceeds
higher than all our hurt disloyally disdains.

Let us not despite insufferable sorrow
forestall new love until tomorrow
tomorrow never better, and when
we mount those taller tomorrows
learning foreign languages borrowed
we will then describe a thing in flight
which once did not readily bend
unyielding unlike less rigid things
so easily snapping off lives
lazily lived at half speed, half cost, now
gone from whom had never so much lost.

Farther than wobbling, weary heart's arcs
yet in misstep still we attain brilliant
arabesques in middle age's breathless
indecision, remains of days grown nearly
night frozen in fitful growing un-together
collapsed into every crowded place, falling
up, circling inwards into who we were
cleft like two hynaciths from the one flower
chosen for that perfect vase
on a perfect table
in perfect pose.

ii

Perhaps we are merely spun about
counterpart victims in our own redoubt
chaotic in unimportant yet lustrous
                              revolving
luminous pivoting infinitely close
of senuously paired binary stars
bright stars if but death stars
                         viral
constant in continuity, together bound
contiguous wherever found
born of Gemini, Geminorum, the neutron
one, and Medusa in constellation
inseparable as a shared, over-beating
Siamese heart, together trapped
                              indistinct
nebulous plasma fields conjoined, recalling
radiant stellar days as ever they are ours
and we wrap round, round
and round each other euphoric

                    spiralling.

SPECTACLE

In each thing there is an insinuation of death.
— Federico Garcia Lorca

One knew.
Of course, clearly, yes.
Yes, one knows an irredeemable mess
yes, it should have been prettier than this
simple and clean;
not largesse, surely
wrapped in cream paper with green bows
but elegantly, without duress.

Now this. It's become a thing obscene
obsessed, practically perverse, nothing
in between.
The disproportionate
scene at Lasserre, as if
no one were there, a spectacle
of disarranged mascara and hair.

It chould have been quick, asceptic
anything but this, the end of the affair.

Yet even in raving, inarticulate speech
she had a certain flare.
One was warned
to be aware of such craving, was mad
to insist, but denial feeds willingness.
(If you had seen her
eager in undress…)

How does one resist?
She was hardly coy and once confessed
she had once been an unapologetic misandrist
and still one would not be spared. One insists.

there is no saving us from our slutty fare
instead, four lives in disastrous disrepair.

My god, it should have been finer
more sanitary than this.
gluttony of over-indulged bliss.
How does one not now seem
prosecutorial, mean?

One wonders how.

Of course, it might have been worse
than this.
          In any case, I see no other way.
One goes about one's day
struggling not to over-rehearse
scissoring one's tongue not to say
one imagined a sweeter end.

Public spectacle is our curse. I despise it.
One cannot pretend otherwise.

Such an absurdity, the delusion
and still one had to see the play
through to its dirty conclusion
our audience willfully appalled.

One knows, incontrovertibly; rather,
one knew.
          It should have held less
hazard, been civil, handsome, more
sane than this.
          Tell me. Surely, you agree.
It should never have happened
                              so
urbane, so clever; decorous and
good.
     So nearly, we.

Reluctant Inamorata

for J

They
(I...)
then you
       [were] fated to disappoint, I suppose.
Not when, but how. The terminal tumble from grace awaited
so near now. There can be no saving face in the end
no taste of absolution, no miraculous, *"If only..."*
with querulous flourish of bluebells and bluebirds
in May; yet, how queer when the wind stalls on the wing.

Would you waste contrite
              future(s) amid wreck and flotsam
righteous in sainthood, cloistered in prayerful, nun-like fright
contrite with numinous intention? Sinner
                 what solution
mourning the annoying, broadening crack in us
your tremulous want of everything almost at once?
I, in the nonce, hardly some Shakespearean king's seer —
though as Fool I have no peer — while you, dear, demure
undaring, neither genuflect nor freeze, flee, or fight.

O do not pretend swooning, heartrending
              remorse not to suffer
treading new lovers through wreckage looted from tear-wept ruins.
Drink in our erotic drowning swept under in this wave confluence
of salt-sweet seas, heave through the shrieking swells.
             Seek no cover.

UNTO BLANKNESS SPUN

Pero se van tiñendo con tu amor mis palabras.
Todo lo ocupas tú, todo lo ocupas.
— Pablo Neruda

Two bore three towards one's bereaved unbreath
wore greedy completion by hers undone, all other
soft, slow ways proceeding against living death
abandoned to former love's barren disbelieving.

Blue June's blooms by fall betrayed turn
downward in clay urns while ancient tunes
play still the same over and again, again.
Hung game and slate; flame and hearth

wood smoke threads its gauze-sheer cloth
moth wings uncaught, retreating. Quick-
swooning, soon the coy, modest departing
funereal drums, caisson in diffident defeat.

My Bess stood night by noon, boon and fate
who fanned hibernal nights into flaming
auroras, and worried not over cloying
sentiment nor vain debating, but schooled

tongued-tied boys by measured halves
no rude, superfluous rulebooks proving.
She bested delinquent, bloody hardly runs
and we, off flying, rose by her good graft.

O not to think we grinning dead do not love
sudden unto blankness spun. None go half so daft.

BIBLIOPHILE

Nothing keeps its promise.
— Philip Roth

Whence, these treatises insistent? Philoprogenitive books
fructuous tomes begot beneath beds, clamming into nooks

covert, undeclared, wended up another wall?
(Do they wish me yet another laddered fall?)

Listen. Linen paper, jacquard ribbons, laid Italian wings
on musty winter air, rude and ruminative rustling things

stack their twentieth hundred onto over-sagging shelves
hoisted while I slumber by conniving, dilettantish elves.

Loose librarian rungs unsteady at each perilous parapet
ruefully soon forgotten, besotted, how readily I forget

snug dimensions of too donnish, heavy-hung rooms
fine bindings beseeching unto lettered leather tombs.

Ten thousand thousand tongues twist fraught, specious pleas:
Read. *Read!* But read as I ought, spineless, no word frees.

COUNSEL OF SHADE

Ineluctably, each regrets apprehending all learned
on the faint, offending far side, but I have little choice
given rare leave to employ an attenuated spectral voice.

Beauty will upend you as we, too, were spurned
flesh, bone, blood, coarse corporeal agents burned
by unhedged bets and the double-blind of decrepitude.
Your proper face refuses to salute you, rude
mocking mirrored informant foretokening the absurd
remorseful, rearward remembrance.
Favourite waiters shrug, no longer attend you
instead bear kirs and crisps to unctuous new
societies of more glamourous things. Chance
a look at what's to be out of reach. Take my word.

Compère, I take no pleasure from our fast, determinate stance.
'Tis a pitious, pitiless speech, that last all-abrogating word.

An Instant Dearly

for JH

...breasts all perfume yes and his heart was going
like mad and yes I said yes I will Yes.
— James Joyce

Long longest keenly acute want's lack of lacking fairly
replete, surfeits of plenty more bountifully than purely plenty
than cornucopias extravagant in plenty where weakest weak wells
utopias of mightiest weak strongest soft so wincing no word or
strength dare speak it.
      Starkly fairest darling rare of red claret glare
reaching there teach me seeking no screeching harlot's careless wares
weeping in wrongest voice your righteous *Yes* deep from lustful noise
for choicest your voice delightful choruses swelling not short to nearly
longest long lengths beseeching further strongly clearly no fear boasting
demurely plu-pluses knowing not never going is barest rejoice
nor sparely speaking wanton ache while ache for trusting you do I
thinking what must unblinking she thrusting sidewise now be thinking
I slink-slaking down cool curve of neck quaking thighs rising
florid areolae undressing untethered caught in profligate unchaste
out-willing heart's bare heady nerve as bold nerve no sheer nerve ought
and never dies so thrilling.
      O not another dearly instant waste wearily
but round steady-hard waist lace insistent, sinuous arms quick, sincerely.

Régate George V

Dimanche, four o'clock, plump on thumping knees
braced babes in paste bracelets raise such tintinnabulation
they incite each party child to wild and spoiled concitation.

Sisters six surround her. Roaring squeal and titter erupts
of all entreating. Plot each their profitable re-nupts.
Birthday girl propounds search and seize.

Babies, babies, she devours them, sweet cakes and teas.
Broad brocades and ribbons, cordons and cups
flouted confections, the much-adored men she corrupts
conceits hang about her in plundered Grecian frieze.

No under-tide, no storm's shouting this unreality disrupts.
T'is what it is plying pretty, parted Parisienne seas.

GREEN GLASS VASE

But little good's to come of a green glass vase
without bright hyacinths, which beam its cause.
In bleak vacancy, as though it were ever thus
it looks an illusory thing from pages of Oz
swipes of rainbow, lost splendour paused.

How to arrange, then, this green glass vase?

Must its empty flute sign an end to spring
forevermore, the goldfinch not to sing
once more? Shall vespers bell no longer ring
as before, and lovers not go wandering
just once more, all dour dowagers cheating?

I dared not watch, not mark fleeting
days course by, months ignored, dimly retreating
nor catch each Sunday table's crowded seating
diminish week by week, so few greeting
our proud door, rust-hinged in March thaws.

Blooms unwilling, whose barrenness under-awes
no good can come again of your green glass vase.

FRANCHISE

      — Louise Glück

It plays out new unto history in egregious evening
come dusk before chilly sun protests no further rise.
Shall mine be yet another voice, thrilled, to despise
in that fatal hour, no refuge from material reasoning?

Aught left, all bereft of beneficent appeasing
do you yet detest the intention of pretty lies
when the hour arrived, when I apprised
each of their ending, every mortal scheme ceasing

pretense? By design there is irrevocable decreasing
of species. How might one deflect the device?
Death wears the mask of Death, no other guise
Death so pleases; yet, who greets him not disbelieving?

Almighty clever I've been with my insidious franchise
banking on that thinnest space between faith and grieving.

GRAVE DIGGERS

Snatch a scent of earth. Smokes. Note the rotten teeth.

One grins at his grim friend by the box to my left
the wry one to my right toes the sod, just beneath
shoulder height, out of sight-line, strong of heft
nodding, silent. Squint eyes of a seasoned thief.
Mostly comic, this rather sinister pair, but deft
on the grift. I hardly twig in false relief
then miss the touch of the pickpocket's theft.

Who can say why we persist in the long dodge?
They take all cards, all cups, infinitely practiced.
High stakes and feigned remorse. We, hodgepodge
at the post, weekend punters, Sunday derby sacrists
horses played out, hope for doping protests to be lodged
then sulk by the gate, ruined, ripping up betting slips.

Not to Shy Away

A most extraordinary thing — everyone knows —
unflinching, preening such pliant, lyrical wings as those.
Beatific, bound not to stand — down —
invested under a plain, ungainly spinster's crown —
feigning no immodest claim to — genius —
scrivening rings round longing lesser legions envious.

What a cunning, crafty — sting — you set
inchoate ambition, deficient pundit regret.
Spun in parallax flax, your fate's own intimations
thwart all dumb destinies of appropriated — aspirations.
Even here — knelt knightly by your hallowed grave —
I dare not dream a life, or death, as one so — brave —

O do not now timorous pretend; 'tis vexedly — your fault.
Not mine, febrile rhymes, but thine pedagogic gods exalt.

Seven Mays in Days

for FD

We are happy. What do we do now, now that we are happy?
— Samuel Beckett

Les vrais paradis sont les paradis qu'on a perdus.
— Marcel Proust

i

Scarcity, thirst; thirst through thin dry desert
expecting neither drink nor sustenance
from parched sands of slight chance. Granular regret
cups filled with sand but not sand, more fine
than talc. Who did not feel its taste in the mouth, dry
dry like chalk? No water, nor air, but rare heat
flooding arid land. Blisters bled salt, our
eyes never cleared, no sign worse than cloudless sky.

I was no Lawrence marching towards the sea
riding to war, gifted a bridegroom's dress
turning historic tides on stolen trains.
Seeking water, we reached conclusion in sand
gut, growl, the stench of tongue and tooth
hump and toe of filthy dromedaries.

Would I had been a booby-headed missionary.
Here, bright scimitars come to sever arm and ear
carve rage from corrupt reason, cut faith to tears;
but I bear no hope, I bring no book of prayer.

Believing in nothing when sun and wind dropped
no triumph to gain, our caravan stopped.

ii

Paris. We raised tents, boxes under bridges.
Eurostar, autoroute, by Saint-Martin.
In December, the wind blows, never stops
until mind becomes wind. There we were
wind-blown beggarmen

                              where once lit a goshawk
with a sparrow in its talons.
                              When March
pushed up the Seine, rose floods of another kind.

We camped in Luxembourg, its ponds crazed.
I cannot recall when spring fully broke
into April. Later
                         gitans, manouches in caravans
returned to Samois, Millet-le-Foret
Chartrettes. The sangliers retreated again
into Fontainebleau. There thrived iris, lily
pear, plum, *cèpe*, chanterelle, all wild good things.

In May, when Jean-Francois held hard to La Palette
the begging was off, then quick dead he dropped.
Investment bankers, chic millennials
took the bet and we were back in business.

It was correct, Saint-Germain with Jean-Francois.
There is regret; his was a proper place.

iii

Walking from Mayfair to Marylebone
we made it a point rounding Soho
and booked Andrew Edmunds near the Garden.
NOMA's high arts are not to be dismissed
but supper by damp, somber Lexington Street
has its special charm. The dirty timelessness
of cart horses, steaming dung and wet hay
hooves sparking stone. It is familiar
like worm woolen socks in worn leather slippers.
We flagged Uber offline to the resto.
There is a network; if you know, you know.

She was…saturnine for two, three years
signaling no alarm. A hell of a shock.
Nor did the closeness help us, so insular
through our time together, too much alone.

The Arbus show at the Tate set us back.
How neurotic, her aesthetic, how fragile
that fearlessness, but there is such a thing
as too fine a truth, the giant in the room.

She left Charlotte Street; I remained behind
staggered, never so psychologically agile.

iv

Our room on Rynek Główny towered above us.
We might have played lacrosse, kicked footballs
down its long hall. Heights as tall as salt mines
dwarfed us and our balcony wrapped the corner
of the building, brightly renovated, and looked
over Krakow's pretty platz.
                                    Boxes filled with red
geraniums separated bars and cafes. From the salon
we watched thick horses draw tourists in carriages.

Then the silence of a refectory. Sacred
prayerfully, as if it were a marriage
we stood before Schindler's shut factory.
She spoke to me of Sehnsucht, of longing
for something beyond language, beyond reach.

Tapered candles in a mine shaft to a cathedral
cavernous, mineral, hopeless breaths
of lost sparrows hanging in still, cold air.
Wearing antique headlamps, we struggled
down and then up steep crystalline stairs
speaking softly of the refraction of Polish despair.

We bought white cloth bags of coarse grey salt
exiting the caves, tumbling into light.

v

Luc pressed oil, herbs, whole garlic cloves
into joints and shoulders of young Alpine lamb.
He turned them over deadfall from the Col
while we drank Génépy, breaths abated
waiting out the dusky hours above Vars
in his gay winter cabin.
                              Their daughter
blonde, feral, played beneath red-checked tables
laid with painted floralpainted of bread and biche.

All ate and drank well before the wood fire
a little tight, her speech too dark to parse.

Leaving, our sledge shushed,running the pass
scarlet faces taking the sting of heavy snow
laughing when a blade skated over the edge
brushing the high top of a great cedar
above pistes brightly lit for night skiers
who serpentined down the runs with flares.

On stretched toes, she reached to kiss the horse's nose
musky blasts of foggy breath unfolding, leaching
into the iced air, a storm shredding around us
then drank Kirs in the bar until it closed.

vi

Our train from Cascais to Compostela
was clean and light in the early season.
From Devon we sailed the channel
skirted dark red rocks along France and Spain
in bitter, beating rain.
                              The sun sat golden
outside the cathedral and the tourists

and the bowed pilgrims basked in flame and heat
before queuing with us to be dazzled under
gilt of Spanish Gothic with Baroque notes
Heredia's organ rebuking through metal teeth
heavy, striated rays and dust motes
descending like shards, specks of gilded foil
falling from a high, ornate ceiling.
                                        It left us
dizzy in our reeling, height to height.

Genuflecting through billowing clouds
spewed by the immense *Batofumiero*
we knelt and were duely contrite.
                              Grasping
at a truer belief, we grieved our doubt
much as children mourn a priest's dabbing oil
at unction before a dead father's godly flight.

vii

From nowhere I spy you passing Opera
crossing with Sophie-Jeanne to Chez Edouard.
So many lunches when we were there
inamorata, in that unreal place out of time
believing all futures were irrevocably ours
without a care, choosing what to discard of onself
for another, what deep in one's marrow must go
when shooting through blue sky arcing arrows
flew towards us.
                        The disembodied voice I hear
is yours but cannot be yours. Where are you?
and I pause, remembering...
                              *Swear to me, swear love
beyond platitude or plagiarism! Swear it!*
That lost day at Madeleine we spoke in schisms
bereaved, no further tricks up sleeves.

Crossing Rivoli to the Tuileries
you reach out, speak, find my eyes — traffic
drowning what you whisper — then turn
disguising that final turning.

                         It sticks, the yearning

dry, crackling vortices of chestnut leaves, sand
across wide streets swirling, lips bitten
tight throat burning.

Le Paradiso Retrouvé

Choked by antiseptic air, re-enchant us wild with old gods' laws
unroused, mild in bootless despair, anchoritic hearts unshriven
nnblessed in livid gall, not less schemes, complots a savage cause.

Uprisen, raucous reanimations of dentured maws
under septic, soulless, soothless beaches driven,
rent by sterile wind, disenchaned us wild with fierce gods' laws.

Dervish savants rave, rant against grasping heretical claws.
Vatic man with ravaged power, acolyte bedamned savour your sin
uncontrite, nor half appalled, not less sustains the savage cause.

Great Grecian beams the tourist overawes
towering giants from hammered marble heads riven.
Buckled earth yet ripe and sweet, re-enchant olden gods' true laws.

Entrails of iron, insidious Metropolis gnaws, gnaws
brain, muscle, sinew, the very atom, gnaws towards Olympus striven.
In pagan insurrection of obliterative fire, no less this savage cause.

Materialist-scientist resequence the strain, rib bones in carbon jaws;
predator, capitalist, repurpose inviolable spires bathed in rood-vermillion.
Re-enchant a cursèd sphere, enshrine in all an infidel God's new laws.
Desire-enthralled, ire engaged, rage — *rage it!* — our sacred, savage cause.

SECTION
X

Sea Rower

...a thousand years, and still I do not know: am I a falcon,
a storm, or a continuing great song?
— Ranier Maria Rilke

By a brush stroke, breach scant between horizon and sky
blade-cut, the blood-smudge slitting blue-back indigo, I spy
that far shore. (*Does it rise to me?*) I daren't claim land is mine; yet
across broken, falling, foam-spitting waves I throw
my bet, for there is nothing left than to row, to vie
towards light. Shall I tread on air, on aether when I arrive
if I attain at all? What universal will, what appalling mind contrives
such apparitions of sea, wind, salt? Where is its inlet
imploring, calling out, receding even as I haul dull oars
seeking a shifting point?
           These shell-truths each man ought
known but by whom has tracked before, wait beached beyond
one final curve of earth. Reaching it, shall I climb up to assess
to reveal, to describe and teach you, *This is the acquittal I sought*
this is the end-sum of so little worth? I can neither foretell, nor rest.

Churning into lunge and lull half spent, intractable leagues to go, I
row. I can but row, chance-swept. There was never any turning back.

DEMENTED GIRL INTO CRASHING SEA

for Fran

But all have touched the same desires
Receded now to oblivion…
                    — Nancy Cunard

Shell scree, unraveling rage wading, who can blame you?
Glad, demented Death splashes stride for stride
beside you towards conch's empty whorl. You'll not shake its echo
nor catch phosphorescent light mixed to coincide
with deep blue-greens of bleak Fuseli scenes. Misconstrued
castle-selves undone on a low beach lose to curling tide.
Who dares round, demanding apologies from the gull-bitch
you now manifest, shrill, unsaved, whose shrieking voice
cries trough to tomb, safe harbour bell fading, feeling the twitch
tugging but half in jest at one sounding dooms beyond choice?
Sand flea on a flattened dune, bonkers scratch without an itch
to hell with whomever seeks substance, or subtlety, or equipoise.
Damn who dwells on nuance in glitchy waves of drowning's noise.

THE SEAL

Round Ullapool harbour's tarnished trawling circus
steel hulls grate white and blue against granite docks
petrol-bright rainbows shimmering thinly subaqueous

masking depths of two flat black eyes subaqueous
half risen among rust-blistered fishing stocks.
Exhorting crowds gathered for their Sabbath's circus

she glares through the landsmen, our jollity subcutaneous
amid the stain-painted fleet, which to port lightly rocks
then starboard, the beast cutting sinuous Vs subaqueous.

Broadly amused, an applauding audience finds it wondrous
but to that great feasting hulk it's all sheer bollocks
plying scraps of chips from her fatuous human circus.

There is no saying whose countenance was more ridiculous
post performance. I suspect its act runs as constant as clocks
bells sounding in a bloated belly buoyed near-subaqueous.

Listen, it's no easy act being puppeted, judged superfluous
dim devices by some subtler Celtic selkie toyed and mocked
by a vying water flea in a pinniped's cloying, predatory circus
cocky carnival barker bulbous and bold, just there, subaqueous.

Wisdom of the Nautilus

for our dead parents

Home-bloomed pitch, wrath in poisoned marrowbone
yearning years scraping gore-scrap with dull spoons
we bore no more new blood than a sparrow's own.

Half-clouded nights under clear-seeming noons
those frail hearts seized harder than quarry stone
through stark, relentless winters

                            no springs, no Junes.

At weddings, in parks among crowds, apart, alone
love's language carved in indecipherable runes
who there were our ken when we clung to tomorrow?

Trauma-impelled, maudlin in pose, our vile melodramas
fictive, fast-fading future worlds from which we borrowed
new words and ways unknown

                            the reticence of Brahman.

Life recoups its cost, its capital in sorrow.
Whence transcendence? Follow Alpha, Beta, Gamma
the vacant underbellies of shells vortices of manna.

Pin of a Head

How, then, achieve absurd ideals of wraithly angels
ungrounded, as it were, in clots of tenantless clay?

Posit minds of no material mold? What an angle
jumps from a skull's diaphonous dream fandango.

Halos hammered, golden-forged, cenobite
attributes beastly mortal cerebellum conceives

drawing what is devilishly implausible from light
skeptics schlep reason, phenomenal man believes.

Thought without form, philoprogenitive rush
movement without engine, no plotted push

any Schrödinger might figure, nor particulate trace
[F]aith, shamefaced, queues in a dullard crush.

Nine ranks of nothingness birth much unholy fuss.
Witness the witless, unwilling carcass unmiraculous.

Das Gespenst

Full kept, our faith in plenty, if never so high as hope,
pressed of cold lead and ink, dressed in RCA blacks and whites,
monotone glories spark-eyed kinder gayly stressed to cope,
impossibilities posed, unlikely maybes at thrilling heights.

Simple things, five cent Sunday plays flown through CinemaScope
crested, breaking waves cascading, hard down the downward slope.
How little worried, they, with aspiration in that innocent age
unknowing no later memory's harkening hash of days will assuage.

Spectres have we thus become, phantoms none could scheme
to be, apparition-stratagems, virtual reams, true fiction all the rage
predictive curves, paper promises, projections we no longer dream
seeking ways unseen. *All sounds are mantras,* chants Buddhist sage.

Streams over stones, we are bees to jonquils, tides claiming shells
monks by bells. Sparest breath of rarest breast grave man compels.

Light Ketch Lost Off Les Glénans

…the sea is a collector, quick to return a rapacious look.
— Marianne Moore

Bright canvas shorn, comber-tossed
lithe little ketch torn, typhoon-crossed
sundered, shredded, wretched
fetched to bed in bleached white coral

which once cleaved colossal, fateful swells
knife-edged under gale, chiding snide gulls
broad, tight sails borne wing and wing
now flown down, bludgeoned, seacocks full

beseech not of your grave widow's frown
brave you, who lunged wave-trough to peak
nor nurse at the hem of her strict black gown
who seeks blame across garden sod and sorrel.

Breathing liquid air and coarse, damp salt
curse remorseless sea's appalling morals.

ASCENDANT

for Bannon

They were ghouls battening on exhumed thoughts.
— Amy Lowell

The center does not resolve.
Up they plunge, plundering putrid earth.

Scourge, ten gone seventy, gouged to ground
gorging on tar, pitch afterbirth.

Half forged

hearts urgent, pathological hammers sound
again. Pound! There!

Hatted wolves!

Rising down to be purged again, unabsolved
rebirthed heaving, red-breathing cardboard men.

Look there! See! They ascend...

The leash men!

VESTIGE CRETACEOUS

...and the White House will be adorned
by a downright moron.
— H.L. Mencken

JACKBOOTS

       JACKBOOTS

            JACK-

BOOTS

    tramp trumped-up America.

Cal Orcko, Charlottesville —

        tracks...

THE KILLING OF HEATHER HYER

Swagger sways to chase
badge, baton, the baying brace
on dark necks unbreathing.

Rage!
      Stay unfading.
                  Rage!
(Freedom raves...)
                Rage!

O righteous mothers, rampage
grieving
            unassuaged, seething
her keen love's avenging
sword unsheathing.

DANTE MOUNTS GARISENDA

And did you have a choice in this? You did...
— Jane Hirschfield

Brit-green Rover en route, Caro buoyantly recites Paoletti's
lists of lavish Italian reds — Nebbiolos, Barolos
dense, round Montelpucianos — and natters of Highlands
passing bright mown lawns under Nantahala's long shadows.

Edging the river approaching Old Edwards, Dante smokes
Petit Nobels, perhaps his worst, though not the sole
Roman affectation, while Carolyne dips ruby-polished toes
into the Cullasaja's frigid push choked with deadfall after snow.

They sip beaded, biting St. Pauli Girls on the inn's clapboard terrace
while their gay young innkeeper, tugging tangled sticky tresses
protests high, humid summer in scorching distress
after a late return from Ascension in cool Prague, *"Czech Paris."*

Along 246 again, he moves in Caro, shrinking from soul-hacked lies
dissembled, then savours La Crème on sepia, areola-taught breasts
thick, dark hair at the umbrous zenith-vale of arched, athletic thighs
her erotic Venus mound, *mons pubis,* and her rolled-back eyes.

Now Malakoff, the 6th again to Saint-Germain and...where?
Puzzling, he pensively recalls Paoletti's sommelier insisting they pair
a pretty Pomerol with rare lamb, indulgent in that oppulent air.
Tonight at de Flore, a Romeo y Julieta. Listless, yet he remains aware

no recent star risen, of a failure to see, counting down declensions.
Debt mounts costing out the preciousness of penny pretensions.

ADJUNCT

Alas! I had turned loose into the world a depraved wretch,
whose delight was in carnage and misery...

— Mary Shelley

Stainless science projects its meta-end to history
come two blitzkrieg, broadside decades. Sub-molecular
engineers, yawning metal-amalgamate avatars
menace forth from their allotrope laboratory.

Invasive, pollinating subatomic machines
diabolical micro-bees dust diaphanous flowers
spawn razor blade petals beneath I-beam bowers
through the cracked continuum. Smocks, jeans

hatch chrome-moly embryos, tinkerers construct
thinking MIT-things in metamorphosis, yielding pure
pseudo-volition, hors prediction, sub rosa. Oppose its will
not, this alien-alloyed titan risen, but kneel as adjunct.

Our progeny shan't doubt it, we die of electronic disease.
Not they, bionic, but our very species decoded, debunked.

EVANGÉLIUM

God himself has no right to be a tyrant.
— William Godwin

The Bible is one of the most genocidal books in history.
— Noam Chomsky

Suffice not, profane speech, claiming outrageous perfection
in hallowed enmity.
                      Blessedly beatific of Him to die
that we may mount the gallery glad at the vivisection.
Let us commemorate Whose demise deigns no patronizing sigh.

O do not mourn, gathered good friends, but celebrate
let us bow to pray, though our happy hour grows late.

Monstrous fiends and frantic mothers pled protection.
Towards Your unholy villainy the living dead dared vie
while You, vile daemon, born of guile and vacant introspection
played King, eater of lips, tongue, tooth, heart…a clouded eye.

Hear us. Preordained man foments no less than whole insurrection
against Your eternal, inverted standing; suffocate on the perverted lie.

Deep in infernal earth, interred beyond mystical resurrection
cherished icon of planetary desecration, you are all We descry.

Pestilence of pride, locust invasion, plague of sinless soul's infection
close that damning, sly, all-divining orb. Die, *thing*, die.
                                 Simply

die.

(Amen.)

FREAKS

Porches crumble, Doric columns peel, still
stumbles Bubba again rich in stoic green glory
ruined stars and bars flying a fool's pride high
binding noose-bound branches of brooding
water oaks bearded in parasitic Spanish moss
thick-tongued as Pawpaw's sap-slow drawl
jawing his offended, awful grey on blue lie.

Clodhoppers clung to confederate greatness
craven, hooded men yet kindle flaming crosses
fated to delinquent evolutionary lateness
born of dollar stores and immoral losses
crackhead jail-birds lacking mama's balls
retching up bankrupt aw-shucks sorrys, ditched
trailers oblique behind shuttered outlet malls.

Long by whirligig and hurricane upended
plywood and poster-covered, gone to bramble
waste laid thick as coal crust, thirteen suspended
tar-paper states your growling yellow-belly
legacy, our crippling cost that chump cause
leaning barefoot in pine-dusted coveralls
layabout laofing on rust-pitted paraquat pumps.

Pig butcher, peanut boiler, tobacco
topper, cotton picker with corn liquor sheen
toothless cud-chewer coon-cornered mean
redneck stacking pickup flatbed haulers
filled with Big Man's migrant-pulled plenty
torcher of tenant shacks down strip mine hollers
glutted hayseed mystery of hooch-rotted genes

fire-hardened yokel rattling Pentecostal snakes
from delta backrooms to creek-bed mud
wallowing in a hilbilly's incest-bred squaller
red men, black men, women whipped; bitches
howling, hounds cinched with spike-chain collars
pleading emancipations of tender mercies while
saltine white, whip-cruel, you couldn't spare it.

Chew on this, boy.
                    By sultry, firey night, cut swine
squealing or gaunt meth-daddy gutted, keeling
every tree-tied, swivel-eyed cur must eat its merit.

CONFESSION

for...

Why didn't you tell me I was in love with you?
          — Fred Astaire *(Easter Parade)*

Years, phantom years, years committing recurrent suicides.
(There persist empiric contradictions no sentient thing abides.)

PSG's perennial collapse; creamy moon now Moscow's own;
baboons in Wuhan precinct nursing egregious, ghastly groans.

Wrists cinched, transfixed by the noose's strained, abraded knot
two men insisted, "*Say!*" I bore witness, sintered iron white hot

and pled what few but nigh recall,

                    a name they shrieked I knew.

When among declining mind's detritus, distinctly into view
abrupt antinomy misconstrued, as if currupt lies were never true

in strode you...

GIRL WITH ROSSETTI-RED HAIR

for SVC

Her hair over her arms and her arms full of flowers.
And I wonder howe they should have been together!
— T.S. Eliot

Florid, radiant pre-Raphaelite girl
one obtained no force to endure
                        splendourous
incandescent whirl who scorched but with flaming curl

were all less torrid, blistering loves our adored Savannah
as once was love
            night's delight-adorned savannah.

SNOWFALL WITH TEARDROP

for JD

Sweet-weaned whelp; fleet, jumping
fellow; sage old soul
                    what yet schemes
your great pumping heart's grey ash?

Who'll redeem dour May mornings when
cygnets sail
                spring's running green Seine?

Hoar-jowled of late, but sore you raced
where long we'd chase, then drink, and howl.

In umbrous doubt, at a corner of my porch
I catch a sound, and spy…the thumping tail.

No one comes
                save Death's Head Owl.

Rhymes Funereal

I hope the leaving is joyful; and I hope never to return.
— Frida Kahlo

Shamans toss bones to twig when drop how, why
loosed, dissembled life-lots dreadful unto die.

When briefest day signs the secret shadows come
we peg them not, our deafness dumb, thick as thumbs.

Scapes of verdant graves, vats of lye, sear of ash
tossing out a Shigatse Buddhist's river trash

no living thing's forecasted sum varies
sovereign, thief, or vicar at Saint Mary's.

By proud stallions pulled, in a rapscallion's mason jar
forgotten, none rest bastioned on some dreamt of star

when furtive Umbra wraps them like a lover
come blithe winter evenings dived cozy under cover.

"Time!" Time, he calls, the barkeep at The Drover
and counts his clock, and nods. We shuffle out; it's over.

Gods assign over whom they'll trod through clover.
It sod, no mortal soul divines however clever.

Prometheus Inbound

Gods —
>   smug-burnished boors
is what I think
>   so I nicked it
and bloody chuffed I did.

Crepuscular pricks, Olympian sods
coddled dicks in wingèd chariots
ambrosia and plump whores.

Piss off! you tell 'im, odds-on squelcher.
No eagle can tame my game old vulture.

WAILS OF AUTUMN VIOLINS

mo sùilean donn (luaidh mo chèile)

But now, whatever spring may mean,
I must grow sadder.
> — Elizabeth Barrett Browning

Johannes Brahms, Ballades, Op. 10
No. 1 in D minor "Edward Ballade" - Andante
> — Glenn Gould

Hitherto, autumn's [monstrous] loss brought romantic pause
among circling, seasonal intervals all but overwrought.
Note, this day, the collapse of another calendar's cause.
None prepare for subsidence, the covert onslaught; all are caught
and few thus wear-worn turn wanton summer eyes
honest in vain hope, from aureate Arcadian days laid waste
by late feints of beauty bucolic glamour dons in fey disguise.
Bright hyacinths grown tall through luxurious days now outpaced
reveal fading height and gloss, which cannot cloak muted decline.
August's clots of finished flowers wither out, ruin wreathes the crown
negligible semblances of June's coronet transmuted now to tin.
Stains blot Venetian turquoise; frowning Helios wends tediously down
orbits in far arcs sepia worlds too parched for words, too anodyne.
Not gilt, but sere-begot, who so adorns a démodé thorn-sewn gown.

Th' Lang Geamhradh

Lang, O lang's th' sleep I dreamt to keep wi' my true love
wi' th' peat bricks' glare glowin' faint awhile, dusted blush an' dim
bearin' th' woolen scarf she wove, an' th' weather'd gloves
flannel an' feather, all wha' save her shiverin' Highlands kin
beatin' brave agin brutal cold where dozy bothie stoves
flare parkie to th' fingertips in narro' vales of fair, fain glen
an' th' colours of th' thistle wane ne'er sae pale o'er th' coves
an' tawny th' tarns dare but yearn for wee trout breakin' by th' fen.

O goodly in grace we'll sleep 'til we cannae keep nae more
when th' fèidh hoove snow-bound heaths to graze an' th' monarch hales
buff as faded heather hidden in th' hills o'er th' ice agin th' shore.
Swathed in down we'll bear December sayin' low, sly Chrissie tales
to coddled, cozy bairns retold, which retellin' misslieness restores
for staunch, aye, 'tis love inures an' nae th' lang geamhradh fails.

Pluperfect

The Boar's Head, La Feuilleraie, Bois-le-Roi

And a stone marks the ground where a sparrow sat.
— Joseph Brodsky

Beauty blooming, all bounty flourishes round me
mounting steps of flower-painted Portuguese tile
counted through my perfect spring garden
tramping towards its perfect cottage door.
Of late, I bend to pluck these perfections so adored
vagrant over seeming endless little whiles
divining who'll not round again to tend summer's
etiolate cottage garden, beloved ever the more.

Brave amorousness of languid doings
declared without the lover's perfect word
my cottage garden's peasant grandeur rings
out rare hopefulness in things one might ignore
a joy forlorn in sighting each fleeting
surreptitious fox, every harlequin bird
pale swan in perfect early morning beating
reed to reed along her river's protective shore.

We swoon, surrounded in my flowered garden
to song, which calls unheard, infracted clocks.
Damp the rose, the willow, the skiff along the dock
and I, as hyacinths spent, forgotten once before.
Yet, perfection thrusts up its doting, as if a duty
new birches trussed straight and still with twine
the copper dial's lethargic crawl towards wintertime
hours tilting by, then lurching, shadow-crossed.

How perfection thrills in my greening cottage garden
where willing barn owl, broad and bright, ululates
from the towering beech by the white and rusty gate
hearing, near, this year's lilting nightingale sing
flicking perfect wings to catch her patch of milling sun
among tumbling honeybees, whose very bumblings sting
with keen quills of grievous words: *Lost, lost...everything.*

Exeunt

What is named glory drifts on air
How can this be the prize?
— Li Po

i

A mark
       the stroke, that word bespoke
starts towards its inexorable smarting.
Merest breath
        letterpress of speech upended
vivid, visceral, unheard; wind whisperer
               scry and tarot
and now you, oxymoron, a joke
           suspended
in air, the off-coloured Somerset quote
no one got.
      You strike at nothing so disheartening
as your striving to snatch it darting
ever away, sweet nightingale departing
fleet-winged, quick, the uncatchable analogic twist.

Who dared aspire, return, not swerve
             never miss
however world-worn, and by earth's edge uncharted
dragons slew?
      Unreformed, rubbing raw nerve,
reborn plexus-nexus of every soon-to-come-due
unlearned modernist hardwired in the germ
not theirs, but yours, this —
         this, at last — is you.

ii

Final stroke
                a last stark, smart word
that half-heard reposte past, now, but again
and again not said better; merely said
                                again
with speech of a different choice
forgotten voices
echoing in a noiseless theatre
directions indicated with charades
inexorable continuum thrumming
towards slow denouement drumming
the low humming
                        inseparability
of light and shade quibbling
on a script's concluding page
(amanuenses in their rage)
until so
            soon, the cast returns
to answer calls and wave, curtains
drawing to a hushed close, and they
march off in proud, propitiate parade
exiting
            one by one along scarred and
plintered boards where
the crushing death scene raged
standing room only and the mooning
audience in breathless applause
                                swoons
through the tropopause, gaping
into a starless, silent, vacant stage.

THE COME

El peor laberinto no es esa forma intrincada que puede
atraparnos para siempre, sino una línea recta única y precisa.
         — Jorge Luis Borges

What to say of heart's impolitic gambles
its trick to bear weight impossible to carry
squashed at best or, worse, left in shambles?

So it is for men of risks and rambles
betting on the come, chancing doom unwary.
What's to say of luck's imprudent gambles?

Peacock on Rivoli, whistling while he ambles
who winks at pretty Sophie, Jeanne, and Mary?
Caboshed in a blink, I'd bet, chauvinist shambles.

Bumpkin by lass plucks berry from bramble
awaits woodland nightfall chill and starry.
What is to say of young buck's hapless gamble?

Observe obeisant priest in retreating scramble
war's toll of soldiers, the dead boys he'll bury;
yet faith's not dashed nor his nerve in shambles.

It shan't foil us, love, with start-and-stop trambles;
we'll run to it, believing best thrashed than tarry.
What to make, then, of roiling heart's great gambles?
(Whole nations toil atop late nations' shambles.)

Etiquette of the Good Host

Though ill-bred Death slips steadily near
I'll not fuss nor be perforce wed to fear
but bear the kindest things to say.

Why cuss the poor cursèd fellow's here?
We set out to find him anyway.

FIN

Coda: The Worm's Art

The minutes are bleeding, bleeding away.
Bartender, make me a tourniquet for this hemorrhage.

> — Christopher Morley

Empowered beast grubs its due
burrowing, the thing gluts and glugs.

Thus am I utterly
                     deflowered.

Sinew scrubbed of sin, there
it shrugs again.
             Listen…

Chthonic fiend, it squirms
                    scours.

O sovereign worm feast
on tepid, meagre heart.

Eat;
    devour:

to

PARIS

True and serious traveling is no pastime, but is
as serious as the grave.

— *Thoreau*

No matter what road I am traveling, I am going home.

— *Shinsho*

C.P. BYRON

Born in Greensboro, North Carolina, in October 1954, Campbell Paul Byron had little contact with his parents and was effectively fostered by a series of African American women he would cherish all his life. Byron attended Guilford College, a small Quaker college in Greensboro. He studied philosophy, flung himself into modern poetry, and briefly mentored with resident poet, Ann Deagon. Byron also studied Buddhism through which he discovered the poetry of Asia and Persia. During a break from university, Byron followed Rimbaud's path to Stuttgart and there spent much of his time working on prosody theory. This exploration would eventually take the poet to Paris. In Stuttgart, he also read Ezra Pound's *Cantos*. When Pound died in Venice in 1972 during a trip Byron made to Paris, he immediately began to sketch ideas for his epic oeuvre.

Upon his departure from Stuttgart, Byron continued at Guilford until later completing degree work in Atlanta, still concentrating in English literature, composition, and philosophy as well as Buddhist and existential psychology. In what Byron tagged the post-Trow world, he read what he believed to be the most important poetic epics to date and over the next decade fashioned various designs for a contemporary poetic epic to mark his generation. Already, he knew he would write it in Paris. So was born *Gypsies of the Unattainable*, a sweeping historical overview lived out in Paris of the late 20th and early 21st century. Byron organized, wrote, and edited *Gypsies of the Unattainable* for more than 30 years. As an expatriate's statement descent into a modern Purgatory, it is definitive for its period. While in Paris, Byron modeled his professional career after those of Wallace Stevens and William Carlos Williams. Byron composed ceaselessly while rising to become worldwide Director of Communications for a conglomerate based in New York and Paris.

During a short trip to America, Byron vanished from Ocracoke Island on October 22, 2020. A witness described seeing Byron's elderly Lab knocked down by waves and dragged offshore. The poet raced to reach the dog but was unable to control the animal in strong wind and heavy currents. Both disappeared in turbulent seas. The witness described a rainbow-like brume above the froth, which then dissipated moments later. The dog's body was found on the beach the next morning, but the island's Coast Guard never recovered the poet's body. Byron's anorak and sunglasses were onshore. His goatskin notebook was in the pocket of the anorak. This is its final entry.

> *In the end, only their shadows behind them had been real,*
> *who were never they; who were never you; who were never I.*

Three years after his disappearance, a former colleague reported spotting Byron across a market in Fez; another claimed to have met him at a *café* in Florence; another saw him listening to fado in a Buenos Aires bistro. None could offer proof of having seen the living poet.

C.P. Byron worked and wrote in Paris for 25 years.

This book is sold at a discount in Ukraine (₴620) in solidarity with the artists in resistance against the illegal Russian invasion, war crimes, and crimes against humanity.